"I see two climbers ascending the mountain, roped together, talking, directing, warning and encouraging one another. Neither berates the other for small slips or mistakes, but they seek rather to bolster and protect each other. The higher the summit, the harder the climb, the bigger the risks. But when they reach the top, the satisfaction is ecstatic."

Magnificent Marriage

Gordon MacDonald

LIVING BOOKS

Tyndale House Publishers, Inc.

Wheaton, Illinois

Fourth printing, Living Books edition, November 1985

Library of Congress Catalog Card Number 76-42115
ISBN 0-8423-3890-X, paper
      0-8423-3891-8, Living Books edition
Copyright © 1976 by Tyndale House Publishers, Inc.,
Wheaton, Illinois
Printed in the United States of America

TO GAIL

whose insights and lifestyle
weave their way through this book.
I am thankful for
the treasure of her company.

CONTENTS

FOREWORD

Irst of all this is a practical book. Those who might expect from a pastor a preachy, sermonizing book on marriage will be surprised. Every page reveals the author's direct touch with practical down-to-earth life. He takes his illustrations and examples from cartoons, newspaper columns, musicals, and the sometimes curious happenings of our daily routine. You can read about toenails and lawn cutting, the bathroom sink and dirty underwear, mailing of birthday cards and overweight, the art of dressing and Senate hearings, the weapon of silence and word missiles, the turtle- and the truce-strategy, party-going and funerals, the art of lighting a campfire or climbing a mountain. Through all of this Gordon MacDonald shares freely with his readers the wealth of experience he has gained as pastor and counselor of a large congregation.

Second, this is a biblical book. It is the secret of the author's reality-related art of writing that it draws its wisdom from the most reality-related book that exists: the Bible. In a most striking manner biblical truth springs alive and suddenly a relationship to our own personal problems is created. Many readers may even be taken by surprise to learn what the Bible has to say about sexual relations, marital conflict, and even romance. Or who would expect for instance that the request, "kiss me again and again" can be found in the Bible?

FOREWORD

Third, this is a personal book. Its most helpful feature lies probably in the fact that Pastor MacDonald is not afraid to relate his own marital struggles, revealing not only his personal victories, but also his defeats. Because of this openness, his wife Gail becomes the hidden heroine of the book and many passages are a touching declaration of love by a husband to his wife. Often people may still think somewhere in the back of their minds that a pastor and his wife are somewhat beyond being human and that they get their children in a sort of supernatural way. This book will put them straight. Gordon and Gail come across so disarmingly human that the reader cannot but conclude: If they too have such problems, there is hope even for me.

Finally this is a theological book in the finest meaning of the word. If it is true—as the author claims—that the key problem of modern man lies in "relationships" and that the answer begins with the healing of the most intimate relationship which exists, namely, the one between husband and wife in marriage, the voice of the theologian has to be heard. Man cannot relate to man without relating to God. Therefore it is indispensable that faith in the living God is integrated as a reality in the counseling process. Gordon MacDonald's book is a striking testimony to the fact that unless counseling is Christ-centered it is never really client-centered, because it misses the nucleus of human existence—man's relationship to God.

Walter Trobisch

PREFACE

The high price we have paid for secularizing our society is seen in the sterility of our relationships. That is why the past few years have seen a growing preoccupation on the part of many people to find ways to define, heal, and strengthen relationships which have been shattered. Among the different kinds of possible relationships, marriage stands as the one in greatest need of attention.

I am committed to the idea that strong marriages will create conditions in which God can make us much of what we are meant to be. The contents of this book convey the dimensions of that belief. My approach to marriage is based on three things: my experience as a pastor-counselor, my studies as a student of the Bible, and my fifteen years of being married to an unusual woman by the name of Gail. As a pastor I've seen some of the worst marriages; as a married man I've experienced the best. But observation and experience are not enough. That is where the Scriptures enter, for they are the tool of measurements for relationships: what is right or wrong; what builds or destroys; what pleases or displeases God.

Any person who tries to be an author discovers that one cannot give birth to a book alone. As my mind sweeps back across the time in which this book was written, several people stand out as having something to

PREFACE

do with its existence. My secretary, Mrs. Dianne Ste-
phens, did the heavy-duty labor of putting the manu-
script into final form out of my scribbled and re-
scribbled draft. Vic Oliver of Tyndale House kept
buying me lunches and convincing me that writing was
a ministry and that I shouldn't be wasting time. And
Mrs. John Becker—a good friend in my church
congregation—kept up a disciplined prayer effort, believing that God could give me the words and the "push"
to keep writing. So she prayed, God pushed, and I
wrote. And I'm glad I did.

Gordon MacDonald

INTRODUCTION

Take a hard look at a few scenes from a "Christian" marriage.

Wedding day: Ken and Carol are striding swiftly up a church aisle. Behind them in the front row sit beaming parents exhilarated with the success of the ceremony. They are proud that their children have married partners in the same faith, that both have high goals for education and career, and that they have never been an embarrassment to either family.

In a few hours, Ken and Carol will call from their motel to thank their parents for the events of the day. Ten days later they will return to a small apartment decorated with furniture half paid for, half given. Carol will work as a secretary while Ken resumes his final year of study at the university.

Wedding day plus three years: Ken's job as a sales manager has paid off, due to a boom in business in the region. Eight months ago, the young couple purchased a ten-year-old home, and now they are well entrenched in the suburban lifestyle. When Carol gave birth to a baby girl! it became necessary for her to leave her job. Ken's position requires that he be a six-day working man. Most evenings he is on the phone or doing paper work. Sunday business has caused his touch with church to decline. Ken and

Carol take no vacations, are deeply in debt to the credit card companies and the banks. They have little time for friendships; what time there is is usually spent entertaining prospective clients for Ken's business.

Wedding day plus five and a half years: Ken and Carol are separated! The latest word is that he is a hundred miles down state selling appliances in a chain store. The earlier boom which made Ken a success became a bust. Ken calls home from time to time, making promises to return to his family or to send a check, but Carol senses that her husband is a different kind of man now; he cannot be trusted. When the business had begun to slack, Ken had turned to steady drinking. He could not face his few friends as a failure, and he could not cope with family life now that his standard of living had plummeted. Thus, Ken was gone.

Carol has gone back to work; she admits to dating occasionally, even if her marriage is not legally dissolved. She cannot handle the loneliness. She confesses to a confidential friend that she had let things get out of hand with an old boyfriend from her church background. They spent a weekend together. God, she says, seems a million miles away. Church would be no help to either her or Ken, she muses. Christians do not seem to understand how one gets into this kind of mess.

Ken and Carol's parents wring their hands wondering where they failed. No one asks about their children anymore; it is too embarrassing. On occasions someone remembers them in prayer, but they usually stay away from an analysis of what happened. No one really knows how a perfectly fine Christian couple could create such a mess of their lives.

Here is a picture of compound disaster. A marriage is in shreds; two sets of parents are aghast at how something so beautiful could self-destruct, and a church congregation quietly wonders how this could happen when people like Ken and Carol seemed to be so sure of their Christian faith. Who could have ever dreamed sixty-six months ago that things would end this way?

The possible roots of disaster are found all through this situation. Some could probably be found in a church which misunderstood the nature of Christian faith in relationships. Thinking that the responsibility of a church was merely to provide the normal menu of Christian doctrine, verse memorization, and youth activities, it could have failed to see that these are not a guarantee for the future. Possibly there was never time to explore with openness the great questions of how people get along with one another and live together.

Perhaps the parents of the separated husband and wife did not understand that the fact that their children were not promiscuous, unfaithful to their church, or troublemakers in the community was no promise that adulthood would be a relational success.

But maybe the most significant root of marital failure can be found in the ignorance of Ken and Carol themselves. It may be that they took their wedding-day love for granted. That they felt love for each other on the way up the aisle was no assurance that they would love each other five years later. The possibility of long-range love at that time would rest on their abilities and motivation to follow the disciplines of relationship, something to which these chapters will address themselves. But even knowing all about the disciplines would itself be inadequate. Many people who have known something about the guidelines of relationships have still crashed upon the reef of marital disaster because following those guidelines became a second-level priority.

Take Ken, for example. There is a hint of the possibility that Ken's loyalties switched from Carol to the sales graph. Is it possible that Carol's loyalties switched also? Did Carol begin to enjoy the "things" which Ken brought home more than she enjoyed Ken? Is that why we read nothing about her insistence that they spend more time together? Is that why there is no attempt to maintain a church base to their home life?

The marriage was dead—or had it ever really lived? Having let their mutual commitment deteriorate piece by piece, they allowed something beautiful to become something ugly. The wedding-day joy was replaced by separation-day humiliation.

This book begins with a simple premise: marital success begins with *commitment,* is sustained by *discipline,* and is evaluated by its productivity *in making human beings something better than what they were when they entered into the relationship.*

For the most part, the world's way of thinking could not disagree more! It resists commitment that is not personally convenient; it ridicules discipline; and it prefers to accumulate things rather than develop persons.

If this is true, a strong marriage is going to be plain, pure hard work. Such a marriage is going to cut across the grain of a culture which mocks long-term relationships. The incredible irony is that in allowing the concept of marriage to weaken, our modern community saps its own fibrous strength. More and more society pays the bill for the very thing it is aiding and abetting. Look with me at a few random illustrations.

Alvin Toffler spoke as a social prophet when he wrote his book *Future Shock* a few years ago. He charted the pressure-rate that was rising in western society as people push themselves to step up the pace of life. Everything moves at increasing speed, he said, and the result is that it becomes impossible to establish any relationship which is both meaningful and enduring. He observed that people today not only utilize throwaway products, but they make throwaway friends. Thus one of the results of life today is that we have a mentality that produces throwaway marriages.

INTRODUCTION

A few years ago it was customary to look at Hollywood and joke about the temporal nature of the movie stars' marriages. Remember the story about the two children at the playground whose mothers were in films. One said to the other, "My father can beat up your father." The second responded: "Don't be silly; my father *is* your father." The tragedy behind that joke is that what was once true about Hollywood is now reasonably true about the social structure of the entire nation. Toffler is right; we live in a society which accepts the concept of a throwaway marriage.

What Toffler sees from the broadest possible perspective, James Hayes, president of the American Management Association, sees in a more specific way in the business world. "Are American corporations helping to dig their own graves?" he asks. He goes on to say that Karl Marx once saw the demise of capitalism as taking place through a revolt by the working classes. Marx, Hayes writes, failed to foresee a growing phenomenon that no one else saw either. The growing "anti-business attitudes of sons and daughters of corporate executives and the attitudes of their mothers."

Hayes quickly dismisses the standard reasons for the revolt of young people against business establishments. What is really at the heart of their feelings is the attitude of their mothers.

There is strong circumstantial evidence that some corporate wives, of whom much is often demanded but to whom relatively little is given, may consciously or unwittingly raise their children with anti-business attitudes.

The AMA president continues with his analysis by suggesting that the modern wife cannot stand the current situation which makes her husband part of a world in which she plays no role and gains no satisfaction. Thus, he describes the growing reaction of wives:

Thwarted, some have become dissatisfied, unhappy individuals who depend on pills and alcohol and show little gratitude for the paycheck which gives them ever changing suburban homes, cleaning women, and empty lives. In a sense they are a cluster of time bombs which can eventually help Karl Marx's basic prediction come true.

Harvard psychiatrist Armand Nicholi sees deteriorating relationships in our society from a third perspective.

In the American home children are no longer cared for by their parents. A home in which both parents are available to the child, emotionally as well as physically, has become the exception rather than the rule. And this is not the disadvantaged home. I refer to where the father is missing and the mother works. I refer to even the most affluent homes. What has been shown over and over again to have *the most profound effect on the character development of children is a close, warm relationship to both parents. Yet our current mode of living makes this difficult to attain.* Parents today relegate the care of children to babysitters, to nurseries, to schools, to boarding schools, to camps, to other children their own age, and to television. We have a society that is segregated according to age. The large families with sustained contact, grandparents, uncles, cousins, and relatives of all ages no longer exist.[1]

We could all gather supporting comments which evidence the deterioration of relationships from a host of sources in our society. The raw data also warns that it is not going to be better; rather, it is going to get worse. Ken and Carol are products of the things Alvin Toffler, James Hayes, and Armand Nicholi say about the world today.

When a man and woman make the decision that they are going to cultivate a marital relationship which will create a super-personality out of two ordinary personalities, they will have made a bold stroke against the contemporary way of seeing things. The great ethical generalization of today is "individuality" at all costs. It is a twisted kind which really is not individuality but selfishness. The supreme price paid for this "individuality" is the loss of productive relationships. When a person surrenders relationship for what I would like to call pseudoindividuality, he begins to grow increasingly shallow in his character and capacity to taste the deepest meanings of life. His individuality is something that has to be asserted, and he must try harder to restate his claim to this individuality each time he comes full circle: he must do more, have more, sound louder, assert greater power, go more places, possess more lovers, and increase the opportunity for sexual variety. Among his enemies are boredom, monotony, other people who wish to assert their style of individuality ahead of his, and most miserable of all—loneliness. It is too great a price, and the common tragedy is that too many pursuers of pseudoindividuality find the consequences of their quest too great to bear, but they find it out too late to do anything about it.

This is not to say that one who commits himself to a relationship loses all of his individuality. In fact, the absolute opposite may be the case. In the long run, his real individuality may actually be enhanced, turned on in living color. This is what Jesus was trying to say in the following verse: "He who saves his life shall lose it; but he who loses his life for my sake shall save it."

It was a paradox that appeared to make no sense. But those who followed him began to learn exactly what he meant. The more they invested their lives in others, the more they began to live. As they committed their lives to others, all of their personal and individualistic traits emerged. Each trait made its own unique contribution to the whole, and each one's personhood became the more pronounced because he gave it away. That is the

A GARDEN OF
EDEN WEDDING

THE STRETCHING OF ONE'S WILDEST imagination could not produce a picture of what the Garden of Eden must have been like. We have some basic facts; beyond that, the whole thing defies the ability of words to express its reality. The garden was Adam's world when God created him.

Adam had everything. He lived in a creative order in which nothing made waves. His work was the work of discovery and exploration. It was the opportunity to use "the stuff of creation" to make things, identify things, and join things together in an infinite number of combinations and varieties which could in turn glorify the prime Creator, God himself.

Adam had everything but a special human relationship. He could look upward, in a sense, and have a relationship with God. He could, in effect, look downward at the animals and have a relationship with them. But something was missing! God put that "something" into words when he said, "It is not good for man to live alone."

The significance of those words is highlighted by the fact that God said the opposite thing about all that he had created. After each phase of creation, the Bible says that God saw that it was good. The word "good" seems to imply the idea of being complete and whole. Each thing in creation was good, but there was one thing that was not good, and that was Adam's aloneness.

Aloneness is the most hostile idea in the universe. It is a word of isolation, and it is alien to the nature of God. God is not alone. Even though he is one, the Bible goes out of its way to point out the fact that God communes with himself. It would be too simple to suggest that God talks to himself; anyone could do that. But God in his triune personality communes with himself: his self-communion is thoroughly satisfying. But man is alone, God says, and therefore he does not have the opportunity for such communion.

It is worthwhile to meditate on Adam's predicament.

He has everything imaginable at his disposal: complete command over the world of nature, the world of animals. He has something to occupy his time, and he has an infinity of things to explore. But one thing is missing: he is alone.

The aloneness is highlighted by what I believe is a deliberate act in the order of things in Scripture.

> Out of the ground the Lord God formed every beast of the field and every bird of the air; and brought them to the man to see what he would call them; and whatever the man called every living creature, that was its name. The man gave names to all cattle, and to the birds of the air, and to every beast of the field; but for the man there was not found a helper fit for him (Genesis 2:19, 20).

I am captivated by that exercise. What is God helping Adam to see in this strange parade? Is God not approaching the doctrine of relationship from a negative perspective? He is out to convince Adam that there is nothing in the universe that can quite assuage the void in his heart for communion. God must have paraded a type of horse past Adam. Adam may have said to himself, "There is a fine specimen of animal—great for a trot on Saturday afternoon. But while we understand each other on basic matters of riding, we do not commune together." Adam may have seen feet-warming possibilities in the furry kitty-cat, but no communion! Perhaps he mused for a moment on the best friend of man, the dog. Hunting? Yes. Communion? No way!

What Adam needed was a helper: someone to come alongside and share the challenge of life. Someone who would feel as he felt, exude joy at discovery, problem-solve with him in a time of puzzlement, create with him offspring who would follow in their steps. There was no one like that in the garden.

I'm quite confident that God brought Adam to a complete sense of relational vacuum in order to demonstrate dramatically to him that there was nothing in the world which could meet his human need to have a relationship. He was created to work best under relational conditions.

It might be well to note the fact that Adam was the perfect picture of individuality that day. You are reading the description of a man who fulfilled the fantasies of every person who has wanted to escape to a South Pacific island and be alone. Adam had it all: he was history's most enviable individual, the original nature-boy with not so much as one irritating mosquito. But he was alone, and God saw that it was not good.

The 21st and 22nd verses of Genesis 2 are among the most mysterious to me in all the Bible. I know what they say, but I keep thinking that there are some ponderous and precious truths behind them. For example, why a deep sleep? Is that simply for the purposes of surgical anesthesia? Or is it important that the production of a woman be a work entirely of God, having nothing to do with the man at all? Woman would be decidedly inferior to man if it could have been demonstrated that Adam participated in the creation of his wife, Eve. But he didn't, and she wasn't.

Then again, I wonder what God was doing when he took something out of Adam and used it to create a woman. Are we being introduced to an amazing fact here? Was God, in effect, dividing Adam into two? Is it possible that the original Adam was more than what we presently mean by the word "man"? I am inclined to be comfortable with that possibility.

Recreating the possible scene leads me to think that the original Adam, a kind of man-woman, is now two: a man and a woman. Adam now has a counterpart with whom he can commune, a helper of his own mind set. And that is why he would cry out when he awoke from the sleep,

This at last is bone of my bones and flesh of my flesh; she shall be called Woman, because she was taken out of man.

The word "woman" in the Hebrew is a complementary word to man. It hints at the idea that the two together form an even larger whole.

Genesis 2:24 has to be removed in one sense from the preceding verse. It is a verse of commentary on that which has gone before. The writer, whom I believe to be Moses, says under the enlightenment of God's inspiring Spirit that these are the events through which Eve and Adam met. That is why (therefore):

A man leaves his father and his mother and cleaves to his wife, and they become one flesh.

The author is actually explaining a present-day phenomenon thousands of years later than when he was writing. He is telling the reader why there is a constant desire on the part of a man to leave the family in which he has grown up and to seek a member of the opposite sex. In each generation a man recognizes in a woman his true counterpart. He seeks to cleave to her and return to the "one-flesh" experience which Adam enjoyed when God gave him and Eve to each other.

I'd like to suggest that there are some even deeper secrets in this text. Moses sees the marriage relationship as a progressive one: two people *become* one flesh; it is a relational process, the product of cleaving. And this generates a number of theological ideas.

First, Adam was excited about his counterpart, Eve, and he was one flesh with her in every way: intellectually and spiritually. There were no secrets between them, and they could discern each other's thoughts. Their one-flesh experience was complete. They did not need to communicate via words; they could enjoy a nonverbal communication which we can scarcely imagine. They could share instantly because, not having sinned, they had no shame, nothing to hide.

When Moses writes his "therefore," he is talking about a later period of time in which there was sin. Now, after the garden setting, there were barriers and obstacles to relationships. Now, a man had to do something that Adam did automatically: he had to cleave. "To cleave" is rooted in the idea of an adhesive; something has to be stuck together. If two things have to be stuck together, it implies that they would not originally have come together unless there was a glue to hold them together. What has changed?

Sin! Rebellion against God has upset the whole design of human living. Sin creates a false hunger not for communion and relationship but for individuality of a destructive sort. Now, *in this day*, Moses writes, a man has to leave, cleave, and progressively he becomes one flesh.

I believe that the phrase "one flesh" means decidedly more than just the sexual act. The sexual act is just *one way* in which the two become one flesh. The result of cleaving in relationship is that two human beings progressively overcome the barriers that sin has erected and recover more and more of the one-flesh experience.

Where have these observations brought us? To the suggestion that marriage in Genesis 2:24 is a faith-commitment to recover as much as possible of what communing man had before the fall into sin. Biblical marriage in its most profound sense is a stepping off into the recovery of the original state of humanness, when men and women were not *exploiters* of one another but *helpers* of one another.

Most people are content to retrieve only the physical experience: to be one flesh on the physical plane only. But the very absence of satisfaction, resulting in the quest for more lovers and varieties of experience, is testimony to the fact that one-flesh means that communion between persons is not only physical but also mental, emotional, and spiritual.

We are not being incurable romantics when we observe a happily married couple who have been wed for thirty-five years and say of them, "Each seems to know so much of the time what the other is even thinking." We may be simply observing that men and women who have made deep, abiding commitments to one another may indeed be in the process of becoming more and more one flesh, that they do experience a tiny piece of the kind of communion and communication which Adam and Eve had before the fall and sadly sacrificed in their rebellion against God.

What was a natural flow of communal process before sin must be a deliberate process after the fall. And Moses outlines it to us in three simple verbs: leaving, cleaving, and becoming one flesh. My friend Walter Trobisch has done more than anyone I know to outline the significance of these three verbs. He has suggested that *leaving,* something Adam didn't have to do, is that act of breaking away from the original ties of parents. It is a negative ceremony which is important.

Leaving must be done not only geographically; it must be done psychologically. And that is exactly what many young people in the process of getting married fail to do. Socially, they may enter into a wedding ceremony, but psychologically they are not prepared to make the great leap of faith into commitment to another person. When crises arise, or great decisions must be made, or resources must be provided to meet the needs of an emergency, by instinct they look over their shoulders to their parents. What they have failed to realize is that leaving should have meant that they cut off the authority and lines of provision in order to begin an entirely new family.

Those who question the value of a wedding ceremony today miss the point that relationships must have a psychological starting point. Relationships which are ill-defined breed many things, including trouble. The value of a ceremony is that it drives a stake into a point of time and says, "Here, at this moment, loyalties and authorities changed hands. Things are different now."

Only those who have the opportunity to treat troubled marriages know how serious is the problem of leaving. When one member of a new marriage keeps looking back at former parental ties, the entire new relationship becomes uneasy. The husband of a wife who wants to continue cultivating a kind of emotional authority relationship with her parents will feel inadequate as a leader. The wife of a husband who has failed to dissolve his ties with parents feels insecure in her ability to trust her husband. A study of the biblical teaching of a child's relationship to his parents seems to indicate that we are required to honor our parents for a lifetime. To obey parents, however, seems to be a command which changes at the point of a child's marriage.

Just as destructive are parents who will not let their children leave. Unable to relinquish their influence over their children, they unconsciously weave ties of obligation about the lives of their offspring. "Why not come and live in the basement of our home until your bank account is large enough for you to afford a home of your own?" one parent says. Another insists that the families get together every Friday evening. A third directs a constant stream of gifts and cash into the new marriage. Often there is a series of unmentioned strings tied to these offerings, and they are usually pulled just as the couple begins to seek independence.

Many young couples who have visited with me before their marriage have smiled at my counsel concerning their ties with parents. But a year after the marriage has been sealed, the smiles turn to frowns, and still another year later, the frowns to tears of frustration. Leaving can be a problem after all.

If the word *leaving* is a negative word of parting from former obligations, *cleaving* is a positive one. It symbolizes the exercise of asserting the new relationship and responsibilities. It is a word describing a continuum, a growth experience. In marriage one is always cleaving—holding on and advancing against forces which would seek to divide the loyalties and fidelities that marriage has to have. I want to emphasize this progressive thrust. Looking back to our observations of Ken and Carol, one can begin to see that this was something they misunderstood. Like many, they thought the love they shared on their wedding day was a sure guarantee that there would be love in the fifth year. But it wasn't, and no one seems to have impressed them with that fact before it was too late. In one sense, one can cleave only enough for today, and then he must cleave for tomorrow on that day. That we have successfully cleaved today in our relationship will certainly make cleaving tomorrow a bit easier, for now we have accumulated experience. On the other hand, it does not allow us to relax and cleave less tomorrow.

The more one cleaves the more "one-fleshed" he becomes. Now it is important to remember that he can become physically one flesh with his wife virtually anytime the two wish. This of course is the sexual act. But the "one-flesh" of Genesis 2:24 is more than something physical. It is descriptive of the full dimensional return of woman to man. That means that one-flesh will be not only physical, but mental, emotional, and spiritual. Together a couple will progressively tear down the barriers which sin has created, and love their way to wholeness. Cleaving is the process; one-fleshedness is the result.

The world has achieved much insight in this business of cleaving. Rarely, however, has it managed to put it all together. Some feel that cleaving on the emotional level is adequate; others are content to cleave on the intellectual level, the level of the mind. Christians would like to emphasize their cleaving on the level of the spirit, that area in which we formulate our values and convictions and hopefully act upon them. There are many who are content merely to cleave on the physical level; in fact they usually end up cleaving to many different people if they are content with only the physical or the emotional.

There is a deepening process of cleaving which we must investigate in full. Set in the context of what biblical data I can turn up, it seems to begin with our emotions, move to our intellect, and finally to our spirit.

The process of cleaving on these three levels is symbolized in the physical act. This side of heaven, only on the physical level will we ever be totally one-flesh. On the other three, we can only hope to achieve deeper and deeper experiences of one-fleshedness. It is a lifelong pursuit, this business of the pursuit of one flesh. And that is what the remaining chapters of this book are about—the pursuit and exploration of becoming one flesh on four different levels:

First, the level of the emotions: Romance.

Secondly, the level of the mind: Companionship.

Thirdly, the level of the spirit: Servanthood.

And finally as a result, the level of the physical: Sexual communion.

ROMANCE: TO LIKE

IN THE PARKER AND HART CARTOON "THE Wizard of Id," a medieval knight with the innocuous name of Rod always seems to be one step behind the tempo of everyone else. That trait is painfully obvious on one moonlit night when Rod finds himself with a lovely princess who says to him:

"Rod, there's something I've always wanted you to do."

"What's that?" Rod asks.

Breathlessly she responds, "Take me in your arms and . . ."

"Shhh . . . hold it," Rod interrupts, putting his hand over her mouth. "I think I heard my horse whinny."[2]

Rod, you blew it! You are apparently always going to be a loser; no romance for you.

With the possible exception of Rod the dumb knight, there is hardly a person in our culture who is not drawn to the idea of romance. We smile inwardly and perhaps even envy the freshness of a young boy and girl who seem lost to the world as they enjoy one another. We call it romance, surrender it to the young, and allow ourselves to believe that romance tends to decline in force with a maturing marriage. But if we have lost it, we quietly admit that we would like to reclaim it.

It is difficult to define romance; it is more of a series of pictures of a relationship than a hard and fast definition. But it appears to center in the "up-front" part of the experience men and women have together. It is the most visible of all the things they do in relating to one another. I think it may include all of the qualities we actually lump together when we say of a member of the opposite sex, I *like* him, or I *like* her.

As a Christian I have often been instructed that I should love other people. I've heard little about liking them. That was assumed, I guess. You do not hear much about "like" in marriage either. It almost seems to be an absurd question: Do you like the one to whom you are married? But the answer may not be as obvious as one would first think.

An Episcopal rector was retiring, and those of us who knew him planned a farewell luncheon. In the after-dinner discussions, I asked him to recount for us what he thought might have been his most speechless moment. Instantly he recalled such an occasion when he had first entered the ministry. He had been asked to officiate at the funeral of a woman who had never attended church. When he arrived at the funeral parlor to meet the family, he saw only the dead woman's husband. The funeral director told the young minister that the two had been married for fifty-seven years.

My friend approached the husband at the casket, and the only thing he could think to say was, "Fifty-seven years is a long time." His speechlessness came when the old widower said without hesitation, "Too durn long; she was meaner than blazes."

Obviously, living with a person does not guarantee that you will *like* him or her. It is quite possible simply to tolerate another person, having worn each other down to the point where the marriage becomes simply a convenience for both partners. The home is relatively peaceful; life goes on with few storms. What has happened is that two people have become amiable room-mates, bound together by habit, by economic convenience, and geographic proximity. But like each other? No! The spark has been gone for years.

I am convinced that wholesome love normally emerges through the relational process of "like." Liking someone is generally an emotional experience. And our emotions are usually the gateway to all of the other relational capacities that we have. This is not always the case. I have dealt with people intellectually whom, at first, I did not like. If the biblical definition of love is to serve, I think there have been times when I loved someone I found it hard at first to like.

But in relationships between men and women, *like* is almost always the starting point. Even as *like* is a prelude to mature love, its death is the preface to the disintegration of love. For when two people stop liking each other, their love will soon begin to die also.

There will be some following my thinking who will resist my fine tuning of difference between love and like. But an artificial separation of the two may in the long run help us understand the different threads of relationship which are being woven into this positive concept of cleaving.

Like is the first of the levels of cleaving. Just as cleaving is a positive and deliberate effort to cross relational barriers, the component parts of cleaving—liking, sharing, and serving—are positive and deliberate. But if you must start anywhere in evaluating these different levels, *like* is the most suitable place. For me *romance* and *like* are the same basic experience.

Like is emotional because it incubates in the region of our feelings. We often describe the experience of feeling in a passive sense—in terms of what someone has done to us. "She excites me," I say of my wife. Or, "He turns me on," a young girl might be heard to exlaim. "I am in love," is a statement of feeling. And all of these statements appear to describe the action of external things upon our emotions. Who can analyze why it is that certain people out of a crowd may call forth pleasurable responses in our own makeup?

Such stimuli may be so forceful that they captivate our entire being for a while. Feelings scream for attention when we come into momentary relationships with someone special of the opposite sex, and we are easily caught up in them.

As in the case of other beautiful experiences, the tragedy of romance has been in its perversion. The contemporary cinema and literature have taken vast liberties with the concept of romance, and for the purposes of exploitation and titillation have often given us either a perverted or gilded view of what it is.

Sometimes Hollywood has raised our expectation beyond the level of reality; on other occasions it has so maligned the meaning of romance that Christians, for example, have fallen into the trap of thinking romance to be ungodly.

Therefore it becomes important that we clear our heads of some of the wreckage that some writers may have made out of the idea of romance and attempt to reclaim what God intended us to experience in the romantic dimension of relationships. If we do not do this, we miss an all-important experience which God meant for all men and women to have and to enjoy.

We have already admitted that romance is hard to put your finger on if you are searching for a definition. It erupts so easily, and it dissolves just as quickly. As I have tried to explore its place in the levels of marital relationships, I have sensed that it performs two services for us. *First,* it draws us together with people with whom there is reasonable personality compatibility. *Second,* romance appears to be a renewal experience which weaves its way through a lasting relationship of commitment. Let's think through these two ideas.

Romance, if it is feelings-oriented, sparks into existence when certain conditions are right. There are special moments in every life when we become especially vulnerable to the stimulation of emotions. It is no accident, for example, that beautiful music, attractive surroundings, and even the mysterious majesty of stars and moon are equated with romance. They frequently crop up in romantic descriptions because they trigger the very emotions we are talking about. They form the climatic conditions in which feelings arise—that is, in most of us except Rod, the dumb medieval knight.

One is not normally brought to a state of emotional receptivity if he finds himself in a garbage dump. He is less than romantically inclined in a hurricane. Place him, however, in a garden on a moonlit evening, and if there is a young woman with qualities that vibrate with his taste in femininity, you have the ignition of romance.

Romance draws people together; it starts things. I have learned this principle while camping. One learns quickly that he cannot lean three logs together, light a match, and expect a blaze. After a few failures I discovered the genius of kindling: newspaper (if your Boy Scout son isn't looking), twigs, and larger pieces of split wood. When the kindling is ablaze, the logs heat up, and before long the campfire is a warm delight for all.

In this sense, the romantic experience appears to be a kindling for a deeper blaze of relationship. It provides the initial heat that may make it possible for a relational conflagration to begin in the deeper areas of sharing and serving.

The analogy speaks to us from another perspective that we cannot forget. Kindling alone will not sustain the long-range effects of a campfire. If the logs do not soon catch the heat and ignite, the kindling burns itself out and becomes only ashes. Most teen-agers have kindling-type relationships which, due to the lack of ongoing, deepening experiences, fail to burn for very long. In our culture we have found it healthy for young people to have a number of such kindling experiences before the final blaze occurs.

Remember that I said romance serves two purposes. In addition to kindling relationships, it helps to keep them going. To change the analogy, consider the common experience we have all had when we pour a carbonated drink. There is something terribly disappointing about going to the refrigerator in the hottest part of a summer day to get a glass of Coke, only to discover that the last person—usually one of the kids—forgot to put the top back on the bottle. What you have in that moment of distress is something which is cold, has substance, but nevertheless makes you grimace in distress. The fizz is gone; the taste, therefore, is rotten.

Romance not only kindles a relationship; it keeps the fizz in it. Sharing and service, the deeper levels of relationship are, in the final analysis, the most significant parts; however, they fall quickly flat when the joy—the fizz—is missing. In a healthy marriage, the walk of two people together is laced by a constant flow of stimuli to the emotions. We inject romance into our relationship, and we get romance out of the relationship. All of our feelings cry out with excitement and each part of us is renewed because our emotions wash over it all and call us from the height of experience.

One further thing about the necessity of romance needs to be said, and that concerns the effects romance has upon people outside the relationship. Romance is the most visible or immediate evidence of love between two people. People see the romantic words, the gestures of affection, sense the enthusiasm two people share with each other. Visibility of love is important. Jesus saw that when he urged his disciples to love one another. The prime way, he went on to say, people will know that you are followers of mine is by the love you have toward one another.

Romantic activity can be a proclamation of witness to many around us of the fact that we share a special love centered in our worship of God. Drawn by its warmth, acquaintances will then be able to view the deeper levels of relationships, and through a composite of them all come to know what God has in store for those who cross over the barrier from aloneness into relationship.

Don't leave out the effect of romance upon children. Nothing makes children more secure in themselves than when they are conscious that their mother and father actively like each other. Esther Howard has written,

Many husbands and wives I know are startled to learn that their own relationship is the most important gift they can give to their children. The quality of their relationships nourishes a child for adulthood and is essential to his psychic health as food is to his bodily health.[3]

Dr. Louise Despert, a New York child psychiatrist, has pointed out that a child's sense of security is derived from the knowledge that he has parents who are happy and united. "If a child is aware of a disharmony between his parents," Dr. Despert writes, "he may interpret it as a 'withdrawal' of their love for him because he has behaved poorly." If these two women are correct, and I believe they are, romance—the most visible part of our relationship—must be kindled that it may kindle, and it must be renewed that in turn, it may renew.

Is Romance Biblical?

Good question! Something within me finds it hard to picture Peter romancing his wife; he doesn't seem to be the romantic type. Dear old Paul gives little evidence that he ever made any girl's heart beat faster. If my thinking on romance were left up to these two men, I probably wouldn't have even started this book. Paul can certainly tell us a lot about justification, but if he knew much about romance, he hides it well. It's not that I think Paul was antiromantic, but you can't help wondering what he thought when he meditated upon the Song of Solomon in the Old Testament. I don't remember Paul's ever quoting from that book.

But don't pass up the Song of Songs without realizing that you are getting an inside picture of one of the hottest romances on record. Emotional expression flows with spontaneous joy from the kind of love these two lovers affirm for one another.

Kiss me again and again, for your love is sweeter than wine. How fragrant your cologne, and how great your name! No wonder all the young girls love you! Take me with you; come, let's run! (Song of Solomon 1:2-4).

Notice the enjoyment of the physical senses in this love scene. Here the lover of Solomon is captivated by one of the same scents that modern women enjoy: after shave—some counterpart of our Old Spice or English Leather. "Come, let us run," she cries out. She is expressing a desire to escape and soar above all the circumstances and intrusions of the routine life. Perhaps she dreams of a picnic in the fields, or running together with the light feet of joy across the meadow on a sunshiny day. What utter abandon she pictures when her inner spirit of love is set free.

Solomon responds:

> If you do not know, oh most beautiful woman in the world, follow the trail of my flock to the shepherd's tents and there feed your sheep and their lambs. What a lovely filly you are, my love! How lovely your cheeks are, with your hair falling down upon them! How stately your neck with that long string of jewelry. We shall make you golden earrings and silver beads. (1:8-11)

Here is a man frankly swept away by the beauty of his lover's face; he admires her beautiful adornments. His enthusiasm for what he is seeing compels him to make promises; he wants to create, to make things for her that will complement her beauty and thus declare his sense of fulfillment in her.

> My beloved is a bouquet of flowers in the gardens of Engedi (1:14).
> My love is an apple tree, the finest in the orchard as compared with any of the other youths; I am seated in his much desired shade and his fruit is lovely to eat (2:3).

These are two people whose emotions are so swelled that words are inadequate to express what they are feeling. They must resort to other images—the strength and beauty of trees, the taste of fruit. Suddenly I understand why a man may call his wife, "honey," or "baby." A loving couple begin early in their relationship to develop a private vocabulary, some of which they would never disclose to the outside world. The words have significance which only the two understand.

If the Song of Songs is any indication, romance has biblical precedent. There is no shame here about expressing unrestrained passion for each other; there is no repressing of one's feelings. There is kindling here. And there is fizz. Song of Solomon is a pacesetter, calling us into the experience of kindling and renewal. It traces both stimulus and response, and the couple who passes romance by has missed the first segment of God's best.

Discovering Romance

There is a curious fact about these three progressively deeper levels of feeling, sharing, and serving. The mastering of the first level makes it easier to move to the second; the mastery of the first and second make it still easier to move to the third. Thus in talking about romance, we are describing something which will ultimately make it easier to share and serve.

I emphasize this because we have to remember that in the biblical view of human nature, serving and sharing are not natural. The force of individuality often moves us to curtail sharing and serving, allowing those activities only when they will ultimately bring something of greater value back to ourselves. Thus, when we determine to shape a relationship in which the sharing and serving will be vigorous, we are reversing the natural process within ourselves.

Since our human tendency is to be weak in making dramatic reverses, it is important that we try as hard as we can to provide a climate in which sharing and serving will be possible. By engendering romance and allowing ourselves to experience it, we are making it considerably easier for the development of the deeper levels.

Part of this effort is to make ourselves likable. Have you ever asked yourself if you are likable? I find it easiest to like likable people. That should teach me that it is important for me to be likable so that my partner can like me to the fullest possible extent.

Likability may depend upon a number of different qualities. These may differ from one relationship to another. Listing a number of them can give us some opportunity to evaluate our relationship and determine our level of likability. In the final analysis, each couple will develop its own combination of traits upon which likability is judged.

Likability Based upon Physical Attraction. A woman in her mid-thirties has come to visit me at my office, and she shares the story of a personal struggle that she thinks is very unusual. Her husband, she says, cannot keep his eyes off attractive women. She speaks of the personal anguish she goes through whenever they are in a group where there are women who are dressed in ways that accentuate their figures. It makes no difference where they are together; shopping, attending services at church, or a PTA meeting. She can depend on her husband to pick out the most striking women in the vicinity and stare at them at every opportunity.

She emphasizes that their marriage is a good one, that she does not feel that it lacks affection, and that they are both committed Christians. What is the problem? Why does her husband's behavior make her feel so inadequate? Is it a sign that he is dissatisfied with her?

My first task is to convince my visitor that her husband's behavior is not that unusual. While it is not necessarily excusable, it is also not uncommon. Most men are quite conscious in any crowd of the more attractive members of the opposite sex. And that is probably true for at least three reasons. First, there is a natural attraction within the being of men to whatever they consider to be beautiful. As to a magnet, their eyes will swing toward any woman who has chosen to make herself appealing to the male eye. Second, there are many women who deliberately dress and carry themselves to attract the attention of men. In other words, they take advantage of the male instinct and enjoy triggering it. But finally, and I lean hard on this, the society in which we live has virtually brainwashed men and women on the importance of a kind of surface beauty. It has taken what was to be a balanced level of sex appeal and attractiveness and, at the expense of other feminine traits, pushed it far beyond the limits of what it was meant to be by God's design. Thus, the feminists are probably right when they observe that this criterion for judging women has been developed at the expense of being attracted to women on the basis of their intellectual capacities, and above all, their depth as whole persons.

This woman's husband has fallen for the line the culture has sold him. While he has been created to appreciate honest beauty, he has gone beyond that and achieved a taste for an oversensualized attractiveness. The two of them are going to have to confront the problem together, and he will have to know how much he is hurting her by his roving eye. In the meantime, I try to point out to the frustrated wife that it is important in her own life to become as physically attractive to her husband as possible. This will make the problem's solution that much easier.

I caution her that I am not suggesting that she enter as a participant in the sexual sweepstakes and compete with other women. But I want her to see that her husband is by instinct and culture an admirer of feminine beauty. The problem he has can be addressed as she helps meet that need by making herself as appealing as possible.

Physical attractiveness is a component part of likability. If we want to be liked, we must think about how to make ourselves as honestly attractive to the one we love as we possibly can. Many Christians rebel against this concept, thinking it to be sensual or carnal. They enter a wicked circle. Certainly an overemphasis upon physical attractiveness can lead to a twisted sensuality, but that can also happen in the lives of men and women who are created to appreciate beauty but find little of it in their spouses. Rather than repudiating this need, the Christian man or woman can master it to the extent that God meant for it to play a part in our lives together.

What is beauty? I have often pondered what makes a beautiful face, for example. I am not an artist and I do not understand structure and configuration. But I do know what is pleasing to my eyes. Over the years I have come to look upon my wife as a beautiful woman. Is her beauty the result of some natural rules of form and structure, or does it rest upon the depth of my affection for her. I think a song in the musical *Cinderella* put it rather well: "Do I love you because you're beautiful, or are you beautiful because I love you?"

A college friend of mine returned from summer vacation to begin classes, and it was soon obvious that he was in love. His friends received a daily barrage of descriptions of her unique qualities of beauty and personality. Little by little we were convinced through the sheer weight of his enthusiasm that his girl friend was indeed the next Miss America. Then we met her, and the old proverb "Beauty is in the eyes of the beholder" never rang with greater truth.

Our evaluation of her was shaped by a cultural standard of beauty; *his* by love. But as we came to know her partly as he did, our view was reshaped, and she became progressively beautiful because we became acquainted. This was the leap of appreciation which our friend had made long before us.

Thus, beauty is culturally defined; it is defined also through our appreciation of the person. But while it would be easy to say that we should always proceed on the latter of the two definitions, that is not possible. We don't possess the human willpower simply to declare something beautiful because of our love and reject the cultural criteria altogether.

Marriage partners are wise to come to terms with this fact. We are ever prone to rebel. We cannot ignore the fact that the old tendency to fit into the culture's view of beauty and attractiveness will frequently arise. Thus, a wise partner in love tries his or her best to reasonably maintain attractiveness on both levels: culturally and as an object of loving thought.

Beyond this it is worthwhile to realize that there is something beautiful about the body that God wants us to enjoy. Happy the couple who have learned the freedom to enjoy the obvious attractiveness of one another's physical appearance. They have tried their best to become physically likable.

Don't underestimate the importance of attractiveness as a reasonable deterrent in a world which overestimates the value of physical beauty. A wise husband and wife face the fact head on that others will use beauty to exploit our instincts and appetites. The more our need to enjoy physical attractiveness is satisfied in the marriage, the less vulnerability to temptation there will be outside the home. We reduce the margins of that which could appeal to our rebellious instincts; we make it easier to be liked and therefore to be loved. There is balance here: love is shaping our concept of attractiveness while our attractiveness is making it desirable to like and love.

What makes us attractive from a purely physical side? Weight, for one thing. It is sad to see a husband or wife who has become careless about weight after the courtship days are over. A cartoon shows a bride and groom in the back of a limousine driving away from church. A frightened look crosses the groom's face as his bride exclaims, "No more Weight Watchers, girdles, and cyclomates!"

A husband shares his frustration about an overweight

wife. "I love her very much and she is a good wife, but I can't get my eyes off the weight and the way she eats. When we go out in public, I know people are looking at her and thinking about her weight. She knows how I feel about it, and I can't stop thinking that she doesn't love me enough to cut down on the things that make her grow fat."

This is a wife who is putting a strain on her husband's ability to love her at deeper levels. It takes greater and greater willpower for him to get past the emotional level of liking her. The less he likes her, the more he must share and serve to compensate. But the less emotional satisfaction he gets, the harder it will be to share and serve, and finally he will exhaust his capacity to keep going at such a rate.

Weight is not the only area of physical attractiveness. Even our clothing and the way we wear it is important. How does our spouse care for us to look? Standards differ from house to house. One young man likes his wife to wear slacks all the time; another prefers dresses. If she loves her husband and wishes to be likable, she dresses to meet the general dimensions of his taste. There is a sad extreme to this, of course, and that comes in the case of a man who wants his wife to dress in outlandishly sensual clothing. Then she must consider God's standards in the matter as well as the message being dispatched to other people about her.

Personal neatness and hygiene are a part of attractiveness. It does not go unnoticed that a man leaves his home in the morning shaved, smiling, and smelling like the Old Spice man. But when he returns, he is disheveled and exhausted. If he spends the evening with his wife and family in this wilted state, he seems to be saying to them, "I have taken you for granted, and I do not think that dressing for you is as important as dressing for others."

I first began to see this principle of physical attractiveness at work in the life of petite Helen Moss, a Presbyterian minister's wife who died of cancer some years ago. As a frequent guest in her home while a student, I did not fail to notice that as supper time neared Helen would disappear into her bedroom. When her husband, Frank, arrived at the door, Helen would meet him dressed in a fresh dress, hair brushed, and a scent of perfume in the air. It was a discipline she maintained. After a day in which he had been out in a world filled with attractive women, many of whom admired him, she was a delight to come home to—not because she had to compete with other women but because she wanted the object of his love—herself—to be something that was also likable.

Another reminder of this principle came in my own early days as a pastor. I found Mondays a convenient day to take off after a hard Sunday of preaching and meeting people. It was simple in my emotionally hung-over state to avoid the razor, the toothbrush, and the deodorant as I hurried to breakfast and the morning activities around the house. On one such Monday morning my wife disarmed me with the following conversation.

"I've been thinking," she said casually, "about why we dress up on Sunday. I mean, why not go to church just as we are when we get up. Why not forget the whole bother of good clothes and such?"

I responded, "Well, we probably overdo it at times, but dressing up is a way of saying to God, 'We want you to have our very best. We want to honor you by looking as neat and attractive as we can.'"

"Is that the only reason?" Gail asked.

"No, there are others," I replied instructively. "We dress for other people. It's wise not to be grimy and offensive for the sake of fellow worshipers. If we didn't look nice, we might turn some folks off and they would fail to hear the more important things we want to say to them."

"So then, what you're saying," Gail replied, "is that

the way one dresses is often a barometer of how he feels about and how he respects other people around him."

"Right," I said, "you've got it!"

Suddenly Gail came around the table and sat on my lap. A faint aroma of cologne tickled my nose; I noticed that her hair was, as usual, right in place. Stroking my unshaven cheek and running her other hand through my oily, unbrushed hair, she said, "Well, dear, if you think that it's important to dress for God and for the people at the church, what does your appearance this morning at the breakfast table say about your feelings for me?"

I was had!

Likability Based upon Verbal Expressions. Saying how we feel is also important to romance. Partners in romance learn how to put their feelings into words. It is as important for one to say certain things as it is for the other to hear them said. Without words, feelings are never solidified, and we are left to guess how the other one feels.

Romance depends upon the frequent and varied expression of love feelings. It was not long after my own wedding that I began to discover the excitement of creatively expressing myself to Gail, my wife. I learned, for example, that a phone call sometimes during the day that had no special purpose except to express love was a welcome relief for both of us. Cards sent through the mail offered a surprise, and I learned to make a stop at the card store to pick out a few special verses which might share how I felt.

It was not unusual to find a note from Gail packed in a bag lunch or in a rolled-up set of underwear if I was on a trip. We developed a set of code words which said things that only the two of us understood. After reading about a man whose wife always sent him off with a special dime with which he could call home if he felt lonely, Gail began the habit of including a dime in every letter she sent. A friend of mine traveling with me in Japan recently caught on to this particular exercise and sent Gail a card. It read, "Gordon is getting lonely; send a lot of dimes!"

If I officiate at a wedding ceremony and Gail is in the audience, we make it a point to let our eyes meet during the recessional of the bride and groom. No one notices that I am telling her with my eyes that she is far more beautiful to me than the bride. Once the head usher brought me a note from the rear of the sanctuary. I could hardly conceal my amusement when I opened up the note from Gail saying how exciting it was to be the only woman in the church that had a "thing" going on with the pastor. She was careful to sign it so that there would be no doubt as to its origin. These are the secret codes of romantic communication which refresh a relationship.

Elizabeth Barrett Browning had this in mind when she took her pen and shared with her lover her own codewords of verbal romance:

How do I love thee? Let me count the ways.
I love thee to the depth and breadth and height
My soul can reach, when feeling out of sight
For the ends of Being and ideal grace.
I love thee to the level of every day's
Most quiet need, by sun and candlelight.
I love thee freely, as men strive for right.
I love thee purely, as they turn from praise.
I love thee with the passion put to use
In my old griefs, and with my childhood's faith.
I love thee with a love I seemed to lose
With my lost saints—I love thee with the breath,
Smiles, tears, of all my life! And, if God choose,
I shall but love thee better after death.

Likability Based upon Appreciation. Romance needs appreciation. Human beings need to know that they are making an important contribution to someone's life. In counseling I have found this to be an area of major breakdown in relationships. I have visited with a number of wives who openly wept as they shared the frustration of having a husband who never appears to notice what they do to make the home a significant place. Women taken for granted, who are unappreciated, sooner or later have to find another outlet for their creativity and desire to please. A few unfortunately find it in the temptation of another relationship. Most will find it in a preoccupation with church work, community activities, or the PTA. There must be appreciation found somewhere.

There is a brightness about husbands and wives who create opportunities to recognize their spouses' attractiveness, their faithfulness to great and small details. Sometimes it happens subtly. I hear Gail in another room talking with the children about how their father has worked hard to bring home the cash that provides clothes, food, and other privileges. She is careful to make the children realize that while she may bring the food from the store, Dad provided the means. It has caused me to work all the harder because I know that the normal routine of my lifestyle is not being taken for granted.

Gail has made my homecoming each day an event. She prepares in advance on many days for the moment when I arrive, and when I walk through the door, the children have been known to let forth with an organized cheer. What man would not want to come home to a family who sponsors tickertape parades in his honor at the front door?

It may be a valuable exercise to sit down and ask yourself what ten things your spouse has done in the past week to make your life different and enjoyable. List them, and find three different ways to express appreciation for them.

This is the place to remark that not only is appreciation important, but the keeping of secrets about weaknesses and problems is equally important. We have all seen the sad example of a man who makes his wife the butt of several jokes: her cooking, her weight, her forgetfulness. Everyone laughs, but she is humiliated. Important to romance is the protection of one another. We may engage in tender criticism in private; but in public, the ranks of our relationship come together, and we are one.

Likability Through "Crazy times." That is what we call them anyway. Romance requires them: times when a couple breaks the routine and does those things that bring a laugh or a memory. A crazy time can be a moment when a practical joke is shared, or it can be a memory that is purchased by going out for an evening or a weekend. In our marriage we may not have many material investments; we have chosen to make our investment in memories, and we have piled up a lot of them.

One day Gail got wind of an unexpected check I'd received in the mail from a publisher. It wasn't a large sum (publisher's checks usually aren't), but she thought that if she cashed it for me, she could use five dollars for something very important. When I left the check for her to pick up, I attached the following poem which would help remind her that only five dollars of it was hers.

> *I think that I shall never see*
> *A girl that's lovelier than thee.*
> *A girl whose touch is soft and warm;*
> *A girl whose figure is right in form.*
> *But one thing must be clear, by heck,*
> *She had better not spend this entire check.*

Maybe it wasn't Kilmer, but it was a time for a special laugh and a memory. Crazy times can be spontaneous if you are deliberately looking for them. But many of them have to be planned in advance. If a couple has children, there are occasions to include them, but there are also times when they should be sent in the opposite direction while husband and wife break free to dote on one another. Good romancing takes time and privacy; we cannot afford to let it pass by.

Perhaps that was what Ingrid Trobisch was hungering for when she engaged in a conversation with her husband, Walter, in an African hotel room. She had been absent from him for several weeks, and he did not realize the toll it had taken on her morale. He kept trying to break through her mood with reminders of the "great ministry" they were having. Her response was:

> ". . . I'm a woman. That's what you don't understand. You can write and talk about marriage all you want, but sometimes I think you haven't even understood the groundrules. For you, I'm just a team partner, a co-worker, a showpiece—but not your wife."

Walter still didn't pick up the signals. He protested: "But Ingrid, after all, we are married. We are together. . . ." And Ingrid cut in to say,

> "Yes, we are together, but always *unterwegs,* en route, never in a relaxed atmosphere and almost never together in the shelteredness of our home."

When Walter attempted to defend his insensitivity to her need, she went on to say,

> "I'm sorry, but my feelings are numb. I don't have the strength to rejoice."[4]

Ingrid and Walter would go on to solve their misunderstanding, and Walter would realize again that what his wife wanted most was a few crazy times, moments when they could refresh themselves by just being alone.

Ingrid was right, and Walter was a deep enough man to admit it.

Likability Based upon Touching. Romance not only feeds on physical attractiveness, appreciation, affirmation, and crazy times, but it needs a certain level of physical touching. This is not necessarily sexual contact, but movements which bring a couple into the intimate circle of proximity, a circle no one else is permitted to enter.

We need to be touched, stroked, held, kissed, and rubbed. Among the saddest moments that I face in counseling are those spent with a man or woman who is alone in a marriage—alone in the sense that the spouse has lost all desire for touch. Lionel Whiston recalls the husband who crept up behind his wife at the kitchen sink and kissed her on the back of the neck. She reacted in an irritable fashion and said angrily, "Don't kiss me while I'm in the kitchen." The husband was heard to mutter as he exited in a somewhat deflated fashion, "It will be a long time before I kiss you anywhere."

The holding of hands while walking down the street says many things. To each other it says, "I'm glad to be connected with you." To the world it says, "We belong to each other and we are proud to declare the fact." A wife sitting next to her husband in the car says by her actions, I like to be as close as I can whenever possible. The enjoyment of a morning good-bye kiss not only gets the day off to a right start, it may reaffirm for the children something they constantly need to know: mom and dad love one another, and that means everything's all right for us too.

A husband who has never quite understood the value of touching writes of his enlightenment:

"The other night we got into bed, and my wife was very nervous. You know, rolling and tossing. I don't know why, but I just started rubbing her back, and soothing her. And then I just held her face to face. I put my arms around her, and we just stayed that way. And this seemed to comfort her quite a bit, and she quieted down and had a good night. You see, I felt this might do her good, and I tried it. Which I'm not sure I would have thought of six months or a year ago. In fact, I suspect a year ago I might have lain there for a while and then said, 'Well, I'm going to have a cigarette,' and gone to sleep on the couch."

Likability Based upon Tenderness. When we're talking about romance, something needs to be said about tenderness. Paul Tournier writes about this need from a feminine perspective when he says:

> The wife has an emotional need which often the husband fails to recognize. She needs to hear tender words, she needs to go out with her husband, to share excitement with him as they admire something, to experience deep oneness with him in the silence of a moment of exaltation. For her love means a permanent high level of affection. This is why she would like her husband always to be with her.[5]

This is the time to pose the question that actually outlines the entire spectrum of romance: How does my partner wish to be loved? To be tender is to ask that question and then to answer it in actions. Too many of us find it simple to love our spouses the way *we want to love* them. I come home for a free evening and get comfortable in the living room with a book. When I go to bed, I pride myself that I have spent an evening with Gail. But I haven't. I have loved her in a convenient way—the way I wished to love. In so doing, I failed to ask the question, first of myself, and then of her, how does she wish to be loved this evening? Perhaps she would like me to accompany her on a trip to the market. "I like to show the other women that you are mine," she says. Marketing is not my way of loving, but it may be the way she wishes to be loved that night.

Tenderness is the sensitivity one undertakes when he asks himself, "What makes her tick today?" And he launches out on a campaign of romance, loving in the way his partner wishes to experience romance.

One would hardly think of C. S. Lewis, the English scholar, as a romantic lover. That is, until one reads his thoughts in the wake of his wife's death. Looking back across the years of his romance with his wife he wrote,

> For those few years, H. and I feasted on love, every mode of it—solemn and merry, romantic and realistic, sometimes as dramatic as a thunderstorm, sometimes as comfortable and unemphatic as putting on your soft slippers. No cranny of heart or body remained unsatisfied.[6]

That is romance, the kindling and the renewing, and it opens the passage into deeper and better things.

Killing Romance

I've always been amused by the bug-killer commercials on television—the ones that show a squadron of mosquitoes or flies happily on their way to a picnic, licking their lips at what is promising to be quite a banquet. Then Captain Raid appears, and the bugs' picnic is over. The expectations of a hundred insects are supposedly ended in a cloud of bug-killer.

There are several ways to kill romance in a similar lethal cloud. The brightest expectations and hopes can be extinguished in a matter of minutes if one member or the other of a marriage follows the directions in one of the following ways. I don't know how many times I've seen this happen at a social gathering, or in a conversation between a few couples—just about anywhere. Delicate feelings are smashed, and romance—at least for the moment—is over, dead.

Ridicule can kill romance. It is razor sharp, and it shatters feelings as fast as anything I can imagine. Ridicule can be sprayed on in a number of different ways. Ridiculing feelings is one way. A husband or a wife coyly confides that he or she is in a mood to do some "crazy thing," and the other person pointedly highlights the absurdity of such an idea. Besides there's work to do. How can we get away for an evening when the back door screen has to be repaired?

Ridiculing attempted affection can be devastating as we saw in the case of the rejected husband in the kitchen. A person is at his most vulnerable when he reaches out to touch, only to have the partner jerk away. To be sure, we have to presuppose that there has not been some conflict which makes someone quite disinclined to be affectionate. How painful the feeling, however, of the rejection of a hug, a caress, or even a kiss. If it happens too often the person who has gone out on a limb will not return for another try.

Ridiculing a mate's attempt to please is another killer. A wife prepares herself for her husband's homecoming by honoring him with a favorite dress, a special menu, and candles. At the very best, he grunts at it all and picks up the paper. He has turned off the switch, and the chances are that his partner will wait a long time before she tries to please him in such a way again.

Ridiculing someone's dreams and aspirations can put many fires out in a relationship. A wife says to a group of couples, "Gene has the dumbest ideas. The other day he suggested that we try saving for a trip to Europe for our fifteenth anniversary. As if we don't have enough to save for. Braces for the kids, school tuition, and a new furnace this next winter—but *Gene* wants to go to Europe!" A chastened Gene sits over in one corner of the room and feels rather stupid that he dared to think out loud with his wife.

Beyond ridicule there are some other effective killers of romance. Take *the unwillingness of a person to express himself,* keeping every feeling locked up inside. No one knows how someone like this really feels; you have to drag reactions out of him with a block and tackle. You do it until you get tired of doing it and look to someone else for response. The man who feels no inclination to share himself with his wife, who never says "Thank you," or "I appreciate this," or "I'm excited to live with you," is going to kill romance in a short time.

The *selfish* person will jeopardize romance also. Thinking only of herself and what she can get out of a relationship, a selfish wife will squander all the desire her husband once had to join in the emotion of a relationship. There's no percentage; she cannot be pleased. Do something; buy something; go somewhere, and she wants to do, buy, or go more. There is no reciprocation; it's all a one-way street. Soon the husband quits trying, and his wife turns bitter. She has been let down.

Privacy together is essential to the survival of romance. A husband may spend most of his free time with his buddies. They are over at the house on Saturdays fixing cars. During the evenings, they are playing softball on the church team. On vacations, they all travel together to the beach. The husband never spends time alone with his wife. She begs her husband for some time when they can go off together, have an evening doing something by themselves. He snaps back, saying that she is always trying to separate him from his friends.

Romance depends upon time alone, secrets shared only with each other, and a sense that each would do anything to get away with the other to some quiet place. When a husband or wife feels as if he or she must share the partner with many others all the time, romance dies swiftly.

To complete a partial list of romance killers let me add the problem of *hyper-seriousness.* It is a mad world we live in, and many of us are caught in the closing vise of pressure from employment, taxes, inflation, uneasiness about the world stability, and a hundred other things. It is easy to become preoccupied and lose the ability to laugh. Life becomes one unchanging color: gray. Romance cannot grow in the heart of a man or a woman who cannot escape the surrounding pressures, for romance is predicated on a smile, a free spirit, and a creative drive to exult in the love of another person. And when that happens, the pipes of the relationship are cleaned out, and two people can renew the great objective of relationship: to become one flesh.

A man went into a card store to buy a birthday card for his wife. He finally found a very ornate one which carried this message: "Your love is worth the world and all its treasures." He asked the clerk how much it was. "That one is ninety-five cents," he was told. The man frowned. "Don't you have something that's a little cheaper?"

Romance is not cheap, but its price comes not in the payment of money. It only costs the giving of oneself in a relationship which says, "I really like you!"

COMPANIONSHIP:
TO SHARE

THESE WERE THE THINGS SHE WROTE *AFTER* the marriage broke up. Where did things go wrong?

When I did ask my husband to spend time with the kids or me, it was always tentative and if I became pushy about it I was "nagging," "trying to get him away from God's work," "behaving selfishly," or revealing a "spiritual problem."

Honestly, I never wanted anything but God's will for my husband, but I never could get him to consider that maybe his family was part of that will.

You can only ask for so long. There is a limit to how long you can be ignored and put off. You threaten to leave without meaning it until you keep the threat. You consider all the unpleasant consequences until they don't seem unpleasant anymore. You decide that nothing could be more unpleasant than being alone, feeling worthless.

You finally make up your mind that you are a person with real worth as an individual. You assert your ego and join womanhood again.

That's what I did. I wanted to be more than a housekeeper, diaper changer and sex partner. I wanted to be free from the deep bitterness and guilt that slowly ate at my spiritual and psychological sanity.

Deep inside there was something making me not only dislike my husband, but everything he did or touched.

His "I love you" became meaningless to me because he didn't act like it. His gifts were evidence to me of his guilt because he didn't spend more time with me. His sexual advances were met with a frigidity that frustrated both of us and deepened the gap between us.

All I wanted was to feel as though he really wanted to be with me. But no matter how hard he tried, I always felt like I was keeping him from something. He had a way of making me feel guilty because I had forced him to spend his valuable time with the kids and myself.

Just once I wish he would have canceled something for us instead of canceling us.

All of a sudden I woke up one day and realized that I had become a terribly bitter person. I had not only resented my husband and his work, but I was beginning to despise myself. In desperation to save myself, our child, and I guess, even my husband . . . I left him.

I don't think he really believed I'd leave him. I guess I never really believed I'd leave him either.

But I did.

There must have been a time in this marriage when the kindling of romance got things started. There must have been a time when this couple dreamed great dreams together. But somewhere along the line of their relational journey, they came to a junction in the road. And without realizing it, each took a different turn. The farther they traveled down their respective roads, the harder it became for them to reach each other across the widening gap. Finally the roads became too divergent for either to recover the original excitement or appeal that they had both experienced in their relationship's first years.

There once may have been feeling, but the marriage died on the level of sharing—companionship. Cleaving demands sharing. It follows in the trail of liking, and it centers on the exercise of two people sharing growth in their minds and intellects. If the fires of romance are well lit, they provide warmth by which the medium-size logs can become ablaze with all sorts of information concerning our inner selves, our interests, the things we believe in, and the creative things we wish to make of our lives.

Never forget that cleaving is a dynamic word, describing the deliberate overcoming of those forces of separation and pseudoindividuality. There is enough of the physical in us to bring people together for a brief emotional and physical liaison. But sooner or later, if companionship does not ignite, the relationship will dissipate and grind to a halt.

What is companionship? I've divided it into three subtopics: *communication, conflict,* and *cooperation.* When we *communicate* we are transferring and appreciating data about our knowledge of things and experience. When we *conflict,* we are comparing perspectives about a particular issue we both face. When we *cooperate,* we share talents and abilities and achieve things which we otherwise would probably be unable to accomplish. All three of these exercises—communication, conflict, cooperation—are a lifelong process and are part of the experience which brings us progressively to the status of one-flesh. As each broadens and matures, our companionship grows, and our capacity to share becomes enormous.

The more I study these three processes of companionship, the more I realize how much they are a keystone to relationship. They are not only important for our marriages now, but we must commit ourselves to planting these qualities of character and personality within the children we will raise someday.

To communicate, for example, means to be able to express oneself. Many children never learn to express themselves adequately; rather they spend many years being squelched—humiliated each time they make an effort to reveal the things they are thinking about. Finally they give up trying. And that surrender paves the way to difficult communication in marriage when they reach adulthood.

To conflict demands the corresponding ability to restrain ourselves from undue anger and violence. Conflict usually draws on the strongest of our emotions—anger, defensiveness, acceptance—and those emotions will always rest just below the surface of our conflicting conversation. If restraint is not exercised, those emotions will erupt and cause great relational damage. Too many children today are not being taught to restrain their emotions, and we are seeing an indulged generation that is going to find it difficult to conflict without giving unharnessed vent to any and all abrasive feelings.

To cooperate is to learn how to submit ourselves to the authority of certain relationships. Sometimes I must submit to those over me in authority; on other occasions I must submit to the covenants of relationships with those beside me. The ability to deliberately submit must be taught at the earliest ages if it is to be transfused into a person's character. When it is not taught, the child becomes self-centered and rebellious, and it is difficult ever to control that spirit. The resulting side effects can be catastrophic when it comes to cooperating in marriage.

So we study these things not only for ourselves, but for how they will guide us in raising our children to be those who can more naturally share and enjoy the fruits of companionship.

Communication

The *Wall Street Journal* prints a cartoon showing an obviously successful businessman sitting on the couch glaring at his wife who has just interrupted his evening reading of the newspaper. You don't have to know what she has just said in order to realize the thing she is concerned about, for he retorts, "I communicate all day at the office; isn't that enough?"

God has made human beings to be—using radio language—senders and receivers. This is part of what makes us relational: the ability to transmit and receive all kinds of personal data. We can form words to convey impressions and discernments, discoveries and evaluations, questions and affirmations. Unlike animals who are limited to a few short instinctive impulses, our abilities as people allow us to exchange an infinite number of signals with each other.

It is pure speculation of course, but I cannot help but brood on what human communication must have been like before the fall of man in the Garden of Eden. Sending and receiving must have been a far more extensive and satisfying experience than it is today. The capacities of the mind to think and perceive must have been virtually unlimited. Along with that, the capacities of the sending and receiving apparatus in Adam and Eve would have been just as unlimited.

While Adam and Eve used language to converse, I'm convinced that they probably did far more communicating on a nonverbal level. Having no secrets, nothing to be ashamed about, the first man and woman probably enjoyed the capacity literally to read each other's minds. There are people among us who seem to be intuitive; they have an uncanny sensitivity to what people are thinking. Wives usually are more this way than husbands. My wife uses the phrase, "I can see right through you," and the disturbing thing is that she can. Those who have such intuition may be giving us just the slightest hint of some of the abilities Adam and Eve employed in their communication with one another before sin started making people fly solo and closed off large parts of their thinking and communicating capacities. The whole area of ESP (extra-sensory perception) may be a residual communicative aspect of pre-fall man.

If we are really interested in communication, we must start with some of the theology of relationships again. When Eve and Adam sinned, all relationships were radically altered; the first shock waves of that breakage came in the communications area.

First, man's touch with God was cut off. That fact is obvious when Adam springs off into the bushes the moment he hears God is coming. "I was ashamed," he told God.

Not only did he reveal the existence of something between God and himself, but he was also hinting at the fact that something had short-circuited internally. His touch with his own inner being was severely limited. Adam lost the control he once enjoyed over all his bodily and mental processes. His appetites and passions would now become his worst enemy instead of his best friend. He could no longer be absolutely sure that his emotions were trustworthy. That which had been a beautifully integrated "whole" was now in a state of general disintegration. Various facets of Adam's being began to enter into combat with others. We see that kind of internal war today in a man's willingness, for example, to listen to the craving of one part of his mind to smoke a cigarette which may bring cancerous effects to another part of his body. Another person desires alcohol with one part of his body and in so doing adversely affects another part of his life. The wholeness of Adam had been shattered.

Adam's relationship with Eve fared no better than the first two relationships. Accounting for his rebellion, he said, "The woman you gave to be with me told me to do it." Adam tried to isolate himself from the accountability of his act by placing two different persons between him and the blame. If it wasn't the woman's fault, then it was God's fault! He gave her to him in the first place, he reasoned. And so the beautiful intimacy of their relationship was also destroyed.

It may be worthwhile to go on and point out that as a result of sin two other relationships were affected: Adam's peaceful and joyful relationship to the world of nature and nature's ecological relationship with itself. From here on out, God said to Adam, the world will give to you of its fruit grudgingly. You no longer dominate it; you will have to overcome it. The convulsions and explosions of the ecosystem today are all residual effects of the great rebellion of man.

From that point in biblical history, man has had trouble communicating. Out of touch with God, himself, and others, he has been a victim of misunderstandings and differing perspectives. But because God loved man, he instituted the great act of reconciliation—making it possible for shattered relationships to come back together again. *Cleaving* is, in effect, a part of the great reconciling act. It is the progressive effort to reclaim some of the communicational capacity we lost, to recover the genius and joy of the relationships that God meant for us to experience.

That is why I keep insisting that marriage is an ideal arena to demonstrate the love and power of God. For in the family, people show the constant and practical ways the love of Christ can aid human beings in overcoming obstacles and barriers originally erected through sin.

The lowest form of communication is physical or sexual. One may immediately disagree, recalling many intimate moments of deepening love and endearment. But the physical level of communication for people is so significant because of the other levels of relationship which are blended into the physical experience. Isolate the physical level from all others on a communications basis, and you have only the instinctive exercise of procreation. Or one may have rape: a one-way form of communication which implies hate, or forcible domination. It is often the act of a man who cannot communicate freely on the other levels of the mind and heart. Thus he tries violently to break through the barriers created in his life.

Many people can communicate on the romantic level as we have seen. Teen-agers do it with a number of consecutive relationships. But communication only becomes more intense and challenging as we move to deeper and more demanding levels of human experience, tearing down the barriers and reclaiming ground lost because of sin a long time ago.

Perhaps we can shed more light on this matter by looking at the Corinthian church. Here is an impressive group of people. They were Christians; they had a large church congregation; and they had access to a number of theologians and other intellectuals. But the Apostle Paul had to deal with a growing communications problem which they faced despite all their credentials. He wrote:

> I appeal to you, brethren, by the name of our Lord Jesus Christ, that all of you agree and that there be no dissension among you, *but that you be united in the same mind and in the same judgment* (1 Cor. 1:10).

It happened in Corinth just as it happens in marriages and families today. People have to be unified in more than just the reality of an organization or common philosophy. They have to be unified in the same mind and judgment.

Corinth didn't have these relational qualities for many reasons, basically boiling down to roots of pride and selfishness. What one learns from this congregational problem can be applied to marital struggles in communication.

The same mind and judgment. Here is the great challenge, to so open our lives and hearts to one another that the bulk of our time is not spent fighting one another but, rather, to blend our abilities and insights so that we target our energies on common goals of growth and achievement. *Mind and judgment:* that is where the communications challenge comes.

There are many reasons why mind and judgment are often out of touch. Let's look at a few of the more common enemies of communication.

Take our *personal moods,* the extension of emotions which sometimes range out of control. Words spoken yesterday in peace can create relational war today; the difference is in the mood of both sender and receiver. In a mood of enthusiasm, a message will be accepted with a positive note while, in a mood of depression, the same thought might totally devastate one's spirit. In the process of cleaving, we put a lot of unconscious emphasis on learning to read each other's moods. The more extreme those moods, the more the relationship becomes one of walking together through a mine field; one never knows when the next explosion is going to occur.

Physical feelings play a large part in understanding communication. We have learned in the past few years that there are tremendous fluctuations in the hormonal activities of the female body. During the first ten days of the monthly cycle, the hormone estrogen, usually called a female hormone, is dominant with the body. At the point of ovulation, however, research has shown the onset of a second hormone, progesterone. The dominant effects of either of these two hormones will depend upon the time of the month, the relative balance of the secretions of the two, and a number of outside controlling factors such as age, fatigue, and stress. The number of combinations is so infinite that we are being truthful when we say a woman can never be fully understood. She can never fully comprehend herself. Being victimized by such fluctuations within her body, her ability to communicate and be communicated with may be intensely affected.

We are in no way demeaning mother in our family when as father and children we have learned to take into account her monthly cycle in relating to her. The code word in our home is "witchy days"; I'm not sure where it came from because it is not an accurate description of Gail at any time. Perhaps it comes from some sense of how she feels in special moments. We have talked about the "witchy days" freely with our children. These are times, we've said, when mothers may find it a little bit harder not to cry, feel tired, or even not to become a bit upset if we are inconsiderate. In most months, we all take delight in trying to help Mom through the witchy days; everyone knows that the rest of the month she is usually helping us through ours.

Communications are affected by pressures in our lifestyle. When the heat is on at work, with finances, or frightening family situations, some folks become non-communicative while others become unusually talkative. Some act with panic; others dig in, becoming more determined.

A woman says, "I know something has gone wrong at my husband's job, but I can't get him to talk about it; he has this weird feeling that he must work everything out himself." What has happened is that a husband has closed his wife out. Perhaps he has learned from past experience that she cannot handle difficult situations, or he may somehow have developed the idea that sharing problems is less than masculine.

It has not been unusual for a man fired from his job to continue to leave the home, dressed for the job with lunch in hand, making it appear as if everything is fine. Weeks later, someone discovers that he is spending each day in the park, at the library, or job-seeking. He cannot open himself up to talk about the turmoil inside.

Guilt will affect communications. It always has. That's why Adam fled from God's presence, why a child who has broken something spends an hour quietly in his closet. We don't wish to face anyone. If someone tries to break through to us and raises memories of past defeats, shameful actions, or resentments, there is likely to be an erruption of anger, defensiveness, or even depression. One cannot think clearly, share openly, or listen objectively when guilt marks his inner being.

A correlate to guilt is the problem of unresolved conflicts. Communication is horribly distorted in the life of a couple where something has been done or said which remains unconfessed and unforgiven. We have all experienced the time when a tiny oversight becomes the epicenter of a larger and larger misunderstanding. When it is all over, we marvel at the way each twisted what the other said to fit each one's perspective. Innocent words were lifted out of context; slightest modulations of voice tone were leaped upon; a few seconds of prolonged silence were interpreted in drastically different ways.

These are just the beginning of a list of forces which can jam the waves of communication. That is why wise marital partners constantly alert themselves to the context of their communication with each other. They do not want anything to alter their capacities to share the same mind and judgment.

The FM tuner in my stereo system has an AFC knob. When the AFC knob is on, it monitors the sending wave of the FM station to which I wish to listen. I have learned that there is a tendency for the radio wave to move just a bit. And so it is necessary to have an automatic fine tuning control to keep the receiver fixed dead center upon the wave, wherever it is. With an AFC device, the signal I hear never seems to change.

good 1/lts

There is no AFC knob that I know of in marital companionship. And that is a great part of the challenge to communication. I must consistently be monitoring the signals sent out by the one to whom I wish to cleave. In some sense we have to communicate about communicating so that we know just how our sending signals are affecting the other partner. In the same way we have to gently let them know how their signals are coming through to us. That means that we are going to have to examine some of the ways in which we can guarantee that we are sending and receiving the strongest possible signal there is in our marriage. What an exciting challenge!

Finetuning
Communication

Communication is the sharing of minds, the blending of our past experiences, our knowledge, our value-judgments, and our plans. But in each marriage that blending is not automatic as we have already seen. If there are built-in barriers to companionship which stem from the age-old problem of the solo-mentality all the way to the various momentary factors that we have just listed, how do we aggressively pursue communication?

Start with the idea of a willingness to share oneself. In order to communicate we may have to lead by opening ourselves up—even if it means the risk of the possibility of humiliation.

As human beings we are vast storehouses of data which have come into us through literally millions of impressions each day. We store our hurts, our defeats, our pressures, our analyses of situations where one gets into trouble. On the positive side, we stack up pleasurable memories, tremendous quantities of helpful facts and insights, and ways in which we have learned to make ourselves and other people happy. All these have gone into us; now can they come out?

Men, handcuffed by something called the masculine image, have the most trouble, as a rule, learning how to get things out. Our society has taught its men to think first before making any commitments, and this becomes true in self-expression. A man is taught *not* to show extreme emotion; he must never show pain or admit defeat. He feels that he has become less than a real man if he is laughed at, left out, or ridiculed. So in the normal run of things, he takes few risks, and reveals only that part of himself that he knows will gain approval and admiration.

If this pattern is left unchanged it creates havoc with his ability to express his authentic feelings later in life. Others find it a struggle to share themselves due to the general patterns often set in the childhood years by parents who cut them off when they expressed themselves, shamed them if they showed weakness, or welded into their souls a horrible dread of saying anything that might embarrass them or the family.

When these kinds of conditions prevail, a person often becomes an intellectual and spiritual volcano. Forces of uncommunicated and unreleased power begin to well up within. If, as the years pass, there is no normal release through communication, these things may force their way out through other parts of the human system. I frequently visit with men, for example, who suffer from heart problems or ulcers. While heart problems and ulcers cannot always be traced to our present line of thinking, a significant number of these people have communication problems, and they find the ulcerated stomach and the pounding heart expressing in pain what they could not earlier put into words. Since the volcano could not erupt in the normal way, it blew sideways into the physical structure.

Part of the commitment in marriage is to overcome these communication blocks, and that begins when we turn over the key to our inner selves to our partner. It may be that what we do is to progressively give over a series of keys as layer after layer of our inner selves becomes transparent to the one whom we trust. The layers open up faster and faster if the one to whom the key has been given is wise in the way he or she handles the information we choose to share.

As we take the risk of willingness and open our lives, we place ourselves in the hands of someone who must accept the real "us." It does not mean that they cannot disagree or even place a sensitive value-judgment upon what we say, but they must be extremely careful to handle us with absolute care. It takes only a few betrayals of confidence or acceptance to erect the walls of defensiveness. Then we redeposit our fears and aches back down in our inner mental vaults where they may never be reached again.

But if we make the vital decision to take the risk and become willing, when we hand over the keys, an entire dimension of human experience begins to emerge. Now we become friends whose minds begin to weave a fabric of co-experience. Perhaps that was what C. S. Lewis was trying to tell us about his friendship with his wife when he wrote,

> A good wife contains so many persons in herself. What was H not to me? She was my daughter, my mother, my pupil, my teacher, my subject and my sovereign; and always holding all these in solution, my trusty comrade, friend, shipmate, fellowsoldier. My mistress; but at the same time all that any man friend (and I have good ones) has ever been to me. Perhaps more. If we had never fallen in love we should have none the less been always together, and created a scandal. That's what I meant when I once praised her for her masculine virtues. But she soon put a stop to that by asking how I'd like to be praised for my feminine ones.[7]

But sharing ourselves takes much wisdom and sensitivity. Having tried to make the point that we should be willing to open our lives to the one with whom we share a relationship, I come now full circle to say, be careful! There are some occasions where one might share too much, or share prematurely. For no human being is equipped to take all the real information we have to give in one sitting.

In our growing relational consciousness, there has come on the scene a tendency to want to spill everything as quickly as possible. There was an old radio game called, "Can You Top This?" Sometimes people in the freedom of a relationship can play such a game, trying to out-share each other. No! Sharing is a lifetime experience; it flows with a natural rhythm in each day as we simply concentrate in being what we are.

Perhaps there are some experiences in the past better left buried. On occasions a partner may be too deeply hurt if he or she were to become aware of events which God has already forgiven and removed. A rule is hard to devise for differentiating between things that should be revealed and those to be covered. Perhaps the answer lies somewhere in asking ourselves if the matter in question could ever come to the attention of our partner apart from our desire to make it known. Will the consequences of what we're aware of ever affect him or her in any way? Will it ever have a possibility of impairing our relationship? If the answer to any of these questions is yes, then perhaps the matter should be brought to light. We can be thankful that God's Spirit can give counsel when we are perplexed about these things.

We must also control what we share in terms of what the other person is equipped to hear. A young husband confesses to his wife that he is having overwhelming problems with sexual lust. He feels better because he has described his problem, but he may have passed his crushing burden of an uncontrolled thought life on to the shoulders of his wife. Now she becomes preoccupied with the "why's" of his problem. Does he not love her enough? Is she an inadequate sex partner? Does this mean that their relationship is threatened? In her inability to handle the information, she has sown seeds of doubt and suspicion in her heart that she may be unable to overcome. Better that he had chosen to open such struggles first to a pastor or a counselor.

Time and again there will be experiences in a marriage where we wish to share something of ourselves but fail to find the appropriate words. I take Gail to a restaurant for an evening that both of us have anticipated with joy. Thinking that I have a clear understanding of what we wish to order, I begin to outline our wishes to the waitress. Suddenly Gail interrupts and abruptly corrects my order. My immediate response, she says later, is a look that could kill if it had a sharp blade.

"What are you so upset about?" she asks when the waitress leaves. Knowing that other people will be looking our way if we show obvious displeasure with one another, I smile pleasantly but force hostile words through my teeth, "Why did you have to interrupt me like that? If you wish me to be the leader and spokesman, fine; but don't correct me like a child when I take the lead."

It's her turn to smile but also to speak with icy tones. "Does your concept of being a leader mean that I can't ever correct you when I think you've made a mistake?"

I respond, "It's not the correction I mind; certainly, you can inform me when I've been wrong. It's the way you did it; you sounded like a mother scolding her child. It embarrassed me!"

"Oh, brother! Is that the way this evening is going to start out? Are you in such a mood that a thing like that can embarrass you?" she asks.

Both of us are angry. It's obvious that we wish the evening to go well so that we can enjoy one another, but an unresolved problem swirls out of control about our heads. We can't find the words that quite bring the problem down to the ground and put it to rest. Somehow I have to find the capacity to express the fact that, like it or not, a strange sensitivity inside of myself has been hurt. I cannot find words which dignify the struggle, and the more I search for them, the deeper the chasm I dig between us.

Gail, on the other hand, seeks for words which express her right to stand up for what she believes. She sees in my attitude something that would better fit the mood of a tired child. But the more she tries to convince me that she meant no harm, the deeper the chasm grows from her side. The phrases just aren't there, and the happiest couple in the restaurant a few minutes before becomes the most miserable. Fifteen dollars spent for good food, but it is a rotten meal!

There is risk in sharing ourselves, and as in the restaurant scene, we will sometimes reach moments of disaster proportions. But if we constantly affirm the fact that we are trying to share ourselves, even when we do a poor job of that, the other may be able to take us on faith and receive us as we really are.

Finetuning our companionship means more than a willingness to share ourselves. It means also the converse: *being willing to listen.* Scattered about the world are enormous radio-telescopes which cover literally acres of ground. Their ears are aimed at galaxies and quasars millions of light years away. They seek the sounds which will give clues to the nature of the universe.

Companionship at its finetuned levels requires people who not only listen to whatever sounds incidentally fall upon their ears in conversation, but who listen aggressively. Gail and I recently attended a performance of the Philadelphia Orchestra and the foremost soprano, Beverly Sills. Having paid eight dollars for a front and center seat, I did not sit back, fold my arms, and doze intermittently while Miss Sills and company did their musical thing. Rather, I strained to get eight dollars' worth. My senses were alert to every sweep of Eugene Ormandy's hand, the slightest caress of the harp's strings, and the magnificent power with which the cello section built a base to each symphonic chord. I listened like a sponge, draining the air of every sound I could absorb.

Companionship requires listening like that. In the presence of the one we love, we learn to distill the overtones of each word. We begin to measure the force of statements, the motivation behind an observation, the hurt behind a protest, and the longing behind a wistful comment. As the minds grow closer together, the conversation takes on deeper and deeper color.

Again I reach back to C. S. Lewis whose beautiful descriptions of his wife include a nostalgic look at her ability to listen carefully and handle what she heard.

Her mind was lithe and quick and muscular as a leopard. Passion, tenderness, and pain were all equally unable to disarm it. It scented the first whiff of cant or slush; then sprang, and knocked you over before you knew what was happening. How many bubbles of mine she pricked! I soon learned not to talk rot to her unless I did it for the sheer pleasure . . . of being exposed and laughed at. I was never less silly than as H's lover.[8]

How C. S. Lewis must have reveled in the hours with a woman who had learned to listen to him. Obviously he did not need someone for whom listening always meant agreement. He had come to terms with her intellectual capacities. He was secure in himself and their relationship. He did not require someone who just agreed with him; he wanted only to have someone who would listen and on that basis respond. And that is what he got in her. How fortunate he was!

In trying to convince us about the importance of listening to the hidden vibrations in companionship, Walter Trobisch outlines the struggle he and Ingrid, his wife, faced one day when he failed to discern what was bothering her. She said to Walter,

"When you said you had no time to listen to what I wanted to read to you, I felt as if you had slapped me. I got the message from you: don't bother me. All night I struggled with the temptation to believe that almost anything or anyone else is more important in your life than I am. And still I couldn't overcome my desire just to be alone with you."[9]

The first quality of a good listener in companionship is the readiness to listen at any moment. This is important because most significant conversations are never planned. They are spontaneous, and no one knows when they are going to begin or end. On occasions, Gail and I have decided that we are going to get away for an afternoon and talk. So we created the time, the place, and the privacy. But the conversation just didn't take off. Why? Who knows? The conditions for a good sharing time just aren't definable. We can only make sure that we are allowing enough opportunities for conversations to be spontaneously born.

A conversation may begin late in the evening when both are exhausted. Defenses are down, and there is a tender tone in the air. Before one realizes it, half the night has passed in talk which will bring a couple closer together than another uncommunicative pair could hope to be in ten years of marriage.

Gail and I remember many such exchanges which began spontaneously. They have occurred on canoe trips, on long automobile trips, during times of sickness, or at the end of a meal. But they occurred when they did, not because they were planned, but because someone was aggressively listening to something another said. A right question asked, an enthusiastic or insightful response, and the conversation is off and running. Many of those kinds of talks are squelched in most families because of pressing schedules, preoccupation with other priorities, or plain old disinterest. In these cases signals sent are resisted.

A busy husband leaves the house for work leaving a frustrated wife at home suffering because an ache in her heart remains unexpressed. That evening he groans to share a deep feeling, to ask a question he cannot ask anyone else, but his wife busies herself with getting the dishes cleaned off the table. Later, each broods about why the other never seems to confide anything. Signals sent were never received, and sooner or later unreceived signals stop being sent.

If spontaneity is a critical point for companionship, then we must be willing to study the signals and, on occasion, be willing to cancel plans, keep awake, drop the newspaper, or let the ironing go. Talking, sharing is far more important.

I have mentioned my friend Walter Trobisch several

times. Once I asked him if he thought the problems of marriage partners were different in various cultures. He admitted that he once thought there were differences until one of his trips took him to an African capital city to lecture on marriage. He thought he would be speaking to a group of African couples. When the evening began he was startled to see that at least three-fourths of the audience was made up of white missionaries. He reasoned to himself that he was speaking to two entirely different sets of marital situations. But feeling that he had come to speak primarily to Africans, Trobisch launched out on his chief concern for African husbands and wives. "The first thing African couples have to learn to do is to talk. The old ways have led them to talk to their brothers and sisters, but never to their spouses. When they become Christians, they must learn to talk with each other." And so Walter Trobisch talked about talking.

At the conclusion of his lecture, Trobisch was amazed to be confronted with a missionary who said to him, "My wife and I had to drive six hours to be here tonight. We drove the entire six hours without saying a word; we had nothing to talk about."

Since that time Trobisch has changed his views. Around the world, the fundamental need in marriage is to learn to talk, and that is what he teaches couples to do. Listening breeds such talking. And when we have made talking a priority, companionship is on the way.

Listening depends not only on the sense of the proper time to talk, but it requires discernment of timing in the talk. We squelch the speaker if we jump in too quickly with responsive judgments, unasked-for advice, or shocked surprise. There is a time when statements should be allowed to go temporarily unchallenged. These are the moments when a mind should be permitted to give vent to frustration, anger, experimental thoughts, or even serious doubt. Little by little we learn that our spouse's statements given at a particular time do not necessarily represent the totality of his thinking. Thus we have to listen to a person's view many times on different occasions to know the sum of his or her thoughts.

A husband's statement, "There are times when I feel like throwing in the towel at the office," should not be a cause for wifely panic. It is a reflection of how he feels at the moment. It needs to be matched with the comments three days later when he expects a promotion. So it is with the wife who momentarily admits that she cannot cope with the kids. Instead of thinking that the family is caving in, one sets it alongside the statement of how well the youngest is doing in nursery school.

Good listening requires that we build a composite view of another person from many conversations, never hurrying to conclusions as the result of any one of them.

Sensitivity to the signals of when a conversation is starting and what is being said is matched in importance only by the obvious necessity of privacy and confidentiality. I am saddened when a husband talks with me about his need to share things and confesses that he cannot confidently open these things to his wife because she is unable to keep them private. "In an unguarded moment," he says, "she will share bits and pieces of a confidence with a close friend, convinced that it will never get further than that." Their companionship is severely jeopardized; by her inability to maintain confidence, she erects high barriers against their ability to communicate.

You have to read between the lines, but it is not hard to believe that Joseph and Mary, parents to our Lord, must have shared with incredible confidence in each other during the months before and after the birth of Jesus. In a sense it was the two of them against the world. What talks they must have had as they contemplated the acts of God in their lives. There must have been tears if some tried to explain away Mary's pregnancy in terms that were less than affirming. But leaning on each other and sharing together, they enjoyed not only a special companionship, but a secure and firm base of a family in which the Savior could grow to be a man.

Conflict

Conflict is a dimension of companionship. Who said that companionship always implied that the waters of relationship would be smooth? The fact is, if there is going to be any viable sharing of minds in a relationship, there will be moments when issues and perspectives are going to be finetuned to such an extent that disagreement will be raised. Conflict is the evidence that there is some distance between the viewpoints of two partners.

Many Christians have felt that having conflict is unspiritual—that it indicates that a relationship is in trouble. On a few occasions I have met couples who claimed that they had never had a conflict. I am always reminded of the statement Dr. Leslie Weatherhead once made about such couples and which Paul Tournier quotes: "Either these people are lying, or one of them has crushed the other."

The issue of conflict has to be faced squarely. Sooner or later there is going to be conflict between two human beings because— as we have already said—we are people with rebellious and independent natures. We have some selfish impulses within us—some of which we ourselves are blind to. No matter how great our admiration and affection for one another, there are going to come from fertile minds value judgments, opinions, and observations which are going to clash. It has to happen; we are, thank God, very different people—all of us.

Take, for example, simple things like the relative value we place upon words. Early in a marriage, a husband tries to extinguish a minor disagreement with the comment, "You're being childish!" Completely missing his sense of perspective, she hits the ceiling, exploding, "Don't you call me childish!" What he has not known is that her father kept reminding her that he thought of her as a child long after she thought herself an adult. The word "child" retrieves from her memory bank all of the years spent building her self-image as a mature person. A bewildered husband raises more conflict than he is prepared to accept because a word carries different meanings.

Different backgrounds raise conflict. Our economic status as children may serve to shape our feelings about the expenditure or saving of money. If husband and wife come from two financial levels, there is sure to be conflict upon the use of the family income.

Blind spots or habit patterns which are important to one but not to another are significant sources of conflict. "I don't understand," Gail says to me, "why you cannot see that, when you say you're going to do something and you don't, it hurts me. You tell me that you'll get that letter written, and you don't. You say you'll repair the garage window by Saturday, but you probably won't. Don't tell me you're going to do something that you don't intend to do."

For Gail the conflict seems to center on my apparently deliberate unwillingness to do what I've said I was going to do. Any way you look at it, I'm wrong. But it wasn't that I lied. It was a blind spot; something at a deeper level has just blanked it out of my mind. I feel stupid standing there having been caught in the blind spot. I may even try to fight my way out of the obvious trap I'm in by manufacturing some new interpretation of what happened. But the truth is, I hit a blind spot, and there is going to be conflict about it because the truth and fact of the situation show me to be wrong.

We conflict if we have different systems of *convictions or values*. A wife believes that the family should be at worship on Sunday morning, but her husband sees nothing wrong with taking the summers away from church for times in the boat while the weather is good. There is conflict, therefore, over differing convictions. Each is frustrated because the other seems so unable to understand the opposite position.

You have to face the fact that there are numerous occasions when we simply conflict because we are operating at *different levels of reason*. Everett leaves the toilet seat up in the bathroom because he sees no need to put it down; Eileen complains because she was taught as a child that a well-mannered person always puts the seat down. The toilet seat controversy brings different images to their minds: Eileen sees her husband as a bit uncouth, and Everett sees his wife as being ridiculously picayune.

Another husband likes to think through his Christian experience with penetrating reason, always asking questions about every biblical claim, expressing doubts and even hostilities about comments which tend to oversimplify the faith. His wife conflicts with him because to her, following Christ means to simply take everything at face value and believe. She has no questions, no doubts, and no intellectual insecurities. Being a Christian is extremely simple for her. Their fellowship, therefore, is often disrupted by dispute over the very matters that should have brought them closest together.

For these and many other reasons, conflict cannot be avoided in our homes. It is a mistake to try to avoid it. I don't mean that we should necessarily welcome its arrival, but our area of concentration should be in controlling conflict—making it our servant rather than our master. If we do this, conflict helps us to grow and not to regress.

If there is an unspiritual dimension to conflict, it is in the *type* of conflict we allow to occur between us. It is speculation, but I tend to think that Adam and Eve had conflicts long before sin entered their lives. I can't imagine two people being created by the Lord without enough differences so that conflict would be a necessary part of their situation. Could Eve ever have offered some better suggestion of names for certain animals than the ones Adam had given them? As two eyes set in our heads give us depth perception, so two personalities looking at the same object or idea with different viewpoints bring dimension to its essence. Those viewpoints present conflict. Adam and Eve simply had to have it as part of their lives. The conflict was not sinful or rebellious; what would later taint it were the overtones of hidden motives, the need to dominate and prove the other one wrong—the expansive air of superiority when in the dust of the competition one has become victor leaving the other vanquished. That is when conflict becomes unspiritual.

Good conflict is *constructive;* bad conflict is *destructive.* The two words obviously explain themselves, and their differing styles are easy to identify when we see conflict's results.

I have always stepped back a little bit when someone confidently says, "I love a good argument; it makes the juices run." Well, I don't and never have. But while I don't pretend to enjoy conflict, I will not run from it if it seems necessary. But many will; they will avoid conflict at all costs—perhaps because they have been disposed of with crushing force at the hands of a ruthless warrior.

Sometimes those who run from conflict think they are doing it in love. They give in on every issue, storing up the resentments and bitternesses inside which someday may explode in an act of violence, leaving, or just getting sick. Even though they think that they are being the more mature by keeping their mouths shut, they are not that virtuous. The boiling hate that steams in their souls is no more admirable than to have let it all hang out. Call him a "clam-up"—that is until the day when he blows the lid.

The opposite extreme of the clam-up is the person we might call the "shortfuse." For Mr. Shortfuse, every little difference is a call to arms. Everything is an issue to be debated, analyzed, and sorted out. He has to win and get his jollies each time an enemy leaves the field with a white flag. Soon everyone begins to avoid Shortfuse, and if he is married, his wife may turn into Mrs. Clam-up. Need I observe that between Mrs. Clam-up and Mr. Shortfuse, companionship begins to shrivel, becoming thinner and more shallow with the passing days.

If we can see either tendency within ourselves and bring it to a resolution, we may then be able to deal wisely with the issues of constructive and destructive conflict. How can they be differentiated?

Good conflict—that which is constructive—helps clarify issues that need more than just cursory thought. In the clash of two ideas, the emotions, the intellect, and even the spiritual side of us with its conviction and values are brought to bear on the real issue. There is a grinding action which removes through conversation all the irrelevant and inaccurate pieces of data that we both thought were essential. Out of the exchange comes a single truth to which we can both agree.

Brooding upon this fact, I poetically reflect:

We two
Brought to a junction of conversation
Two glimpses, dimensions, and feelings
Of a single reality.
Volume increased,
Faces reddened,
And for a moment
We stood like gladiators
Dueling to the very death.
Integrity and Dignity seemed at first to be at stake
But as we parried and thrust
With reason, wit, and turn of words,
A remarkable thing occurred.
For our momentary distance
Led us both
To a new birth of understanding.

Out of argument came a polished
Insight which we two now treasure
And would have missed
Had we been afraid
To trust our friendship
To challenging conflict.

Constructive conflict also encourages and develops maturity. In the test of opinions we are forced to face ourselves as we really are. Gail calls me to attention about some insensitive action on my part. I listen, and perhaps I even debate the point hoping to explain my thinking. But if I am in a frame of mind to learn, I may suddenly discover in the verbal trade that she has pointed out something worth thinking about. I come out of the conflict with new insights about myself. I grow up just a bit more.

"I like fighting," someone says with a romantic air, "because when the fighting is over, the making up is fantastic." If you've heard that as many times as I have, you groan as I do. But take a second look. There may be truth to the statement after all. Constructive conflict cleans out the tubes of the relationship. Things which have been lying dormant are finally picked up and tossed in the air. If there is an ability to deal with them truthfully and bring them to resolution, the making up *will be* fantastic. It is fantastic because there is an explosion of relief. We're glad that's over with; it's been said, and now we can get on to the other business.

Take a quick look at destructive conflict. It obviously does not build relationships; it whittles them down. Conflict becomes destructive when the parties in question point their weapons at each other rather than at the issue. Note the subtle differences between the two statements, "*You* make me so mad," and "*What you have done* makes me very angry." The weapons have swiveled from one target to another.

Now we bring into view the kinds of things most

people associate with conflict between husbands and wives: accusations, name-calling, strident tones, and volume heard all over the neighborhood.

This is the kind of conflict in which someone has to win. They will not call it quits until the other waves a flag of unconditional surrender. Little by little, personalities are destroyed, and one or both people come out of the relationship beaten and crushed. The relationship is cheapened, and companionship is something of the past.

Unresolved and destructive conflicts make a mess out of lives. A recent *Reader's Digest* article makes the point:

> In Houston, Texas, an angry businessman, after a furious quarrel with his wife, dashed out to his car yelling, "You may never see me again." He was right. Speeding recklessly down the highway, he ran head-on into a truck and was killed. Researchers in Houston, who have interviewed families of persons who died at the wheel in car accidents, found that more than half have had serious personal conflict in the twenty-four hours preceding death.[10]

"Destructive" is obviously a good word for the kind of conflict that has such an effect.

The Origins of Destructive Conflict

If we do not master constructive conflict, destructive conflict will master us. To insure that this not happen, we must be willing to honestly inquire into some of the roots of those things which pave a freeway toward destructive tendencies in marriage. I have to confess frankly that it is much easier to take a hard look at these roots on paper, to write about them, or even to speak about them. But it never becomes easier to analyze them when I am in the middle of the actual heat of marital debate. What counselor has not said to himself in the process of personal conflict, "If this were any other person but my wife (or husband as the case may be), I'd know exactly how to handle the situation."

If knowledge were the key to overcoming all destructive conflicts, psychologists and psychiatrists would lead the list as the happiest people in the world. But a look at the statistics shows them to rank among the highest in divorces and suicides in the United States. Why? Because the roots of inner and interpersonal conflict are not intellectual; they are matters of the inner spirit which clog the mind and make constructive sharing a seriously impaired capacity apart from the freedom found in the spirit of Jesus Christ.

Pride is at the root of almost all marital conflict. Pride is the part of us that cannot face being wrong. Thus we will not accept criticism, easily evaluate facts which suggest that we hold the wrong opinion, or allow for the possibility that there simply may be times when our partner is right and we are dead wrong. As long as being the strongest, the best, and the "rightest" is top priority, conflict will be destructive. Pride suggests that I am more important than the relationship, and that is all out of harmony with the original vows of Christian commitment which said that the relationship is more important than the individual.

The woman possessed of crippling pride cannot stand for her husband to make the slightest negative comment about the way she cooks or keeps her home. Pride marks the character of a man who cannot be told that the way he relates to his children may be unwise. For both, the greatest enemy of their lives may be that inability to look inward and face the conclusion, "I've made a mistake." What a burden is lifted when one no longer has to be right about everything.

A number of years as a Christian pastor has convinced me that the person who does not have to be proven right at all costs is among the most liberated of all human beings. Isn't it remarkable how we all avoid the man or woman who has a hair trigger on all issues? In marriage a husband with a wife like that tiptoes through all areas of potential disagreement. She may wonder why he rarely expresses himself, while the answer may lie in her devastating retaliation when she feels her pride being threatened by the truth.

Selfishness is another breeding ground for conflict. This person has the vague idea that the world centers on him. It is all right for him to come home ten minutes later than supper was scheduled, but no one can keep him waiting. His language is brusque and biting; his use of money and time are for his convenience. He demands by his insensitivity that all others make their world conform to him.

Over the years, I have increasingly realized my own insensitivity. A conflict some years ago brought a delightful change in style to my own life. I had failed to cut the lawn for the second consecutive week, and Gail was upset with me. At the time I saw no need for her to feel the way she did. Trying, however, to be sensitive, I began to become aware of something that was frighteningly important but totally missing in my comprehension of companionship.

My family had moved frequently during my childhood. Frankly, I never defined "home" as a house. "Home" to me was the present set of relationships, friends that one had wherever he lived. Unconsciously I took little pride and gave even less attention to the house where we lived. It was a place to eat and sleep, to meet other members of the family. It was a house, but I never thought of it as a "home." On the other hand, Gail had a place she called a home. She had lived in the same home for almost twenty years. Even the structure was important to her because it was her place of growing up. A happy girlhood home had caused her to dream of the day when she would have her own home. In contrast, all I ever dreamed about was owning a new car.

What taught me a dramatic lesson was my sudden awareness that I had become incredibly selfish in my perspective of matters in our home. I began to realize that I wanted my wife to be an admiring critic of my sermons. They were the peak moments of my personal ministry and creativity. I wanted her to listen, even to take notes. I wanted her evaluation and, hopefully, her affirmation. It had never occurred to me, however, that she also had a "sermon" to preach. Her pulpit was our house. She preached her sermon when she cooked a meal, arranged an artistic centerpiece, kept the house neat, and planted flowers in the front yard.

When I failed to show interest in cutting the lawn, or threw my sportcoat over the front doorknob, or left my toilet articles on the bathroom sink, I was being selfish, doing the very thing that would have shattered me if she had done it to me. I was disinterested in her "sermon." "O God," I prayed, "forgive me for being so insensitive to the things that are important to my wife; train me to understand the importance of hearing and enjoying the sermons in her life."

Quietly I vowed to myself that Gail would never pick up another sportcoat or dirty piece of underwear, that she would never find my hairbrush on the bathroom sink, and that she would never have to ask me again to cut the lawn. I've scored pretty heavily on the first two counts. The crowning part of my achievement of a new domestic lifestyle was that within a few months, my new posture of neatness became not a discipline but a habit. Today it would make me restless to go to bed without having hung up my clothes. My new sensitivity avoided many, many destructive conflicts.

Destructive conflict can arise over *confusion of goals and convictions in marriage.* We will often conflict, I suppose, over things like money, use of time, kinds of friends, or even behavior patterns. The conflict will be constructive if we have a basic measurement to which we both submit. In our home the adage "Convictions always supersede preference" speaks to the point. If we have a conviction about spending too much money on luxury items for our home, we can constructively conflict over whether a thing is necessary or not. But if we have no conviction, the same argument can become destructive as we argue purely from selfish desire. Here again, the need for a commitment to biblical foundations becomes important. Lives submitted to the Scriptures leave little room for conflict which tears people apart.

Conflict of a destructive sort breeds quickly if there is an inability to accept our partner as he really is. A dangerous marital game is called "Why can't you be like . . . ?" It can work with effective force from both sides. The wife who knows that her husband is always comparing her appearance with another woman is hurt just as badly as the man who knows that he is being compared with another man who can afford to take his family to Bermuda every spring vacation.

It was Keith Miller who first made me aware of this fatal cancer of relationship. Recalling his first attempts to bring his wife, Mary Allen, to the commitment he had experienced with God, he began to realize how unwilling he was to accept her as she really was. He notes, "In retrospect, I think Mary Allen's vision of a husband was a perfectly balanced blend of big John Wayne, Jack Parr, and Father Flanagan. But in all honesty, I think my premarital vision of an ideal wife was probably a combination of St. Theresa, Elizabeth Taylor, and . . . Betty Crocker." Like many of us, Miller formed new depths to their companionship when he learned to love his wife for exactly what she was and not some plastic model of what he wished for her to be. Perhaps it was the same lesson a woman indicated she had learned when she changed her prayer, "O Lord, you love him and I'll change him," to "O Lord, you change him and I'll love him."

Note *suspicion* as a breeding ground for destructive conflict. A husband or wife who was hurt, let down, lied to by parents or by earlier companions may have a difficult time totally trusting his or her partner. Destructive conflict breeds rapidly when we refuse to trust one another. Dr. Jay Adams gives an excellent picture of its tentacles:

Tom and Jill sat across the desk. She said in the most bitter terms, "I am absolutely certain that this husband of mine is cheating on me; he's been stealing money from his overtime pay. I know he's been stealing money. And I want to know what he's been doing with it." *She had been holding this over his head for the last four or five months,* ever since she discovered it had been going on. Turning to her husband, the counselor said, "Tom, where did the money go; did you really take it?" Slowly he reached into his pocket, pulled out his wallet, dug down into the secret compartment, and replied, "It's all here," as he pulled it out and threw it down on the desk. "I've been saving it for our anniversary for a special time for Jill."[11]

There is no hope for a relationship to grow as long as one partner holds a shred of suspicion over the other. Mistrust is a killer to companionship, and the conflict which arises out of it destroys with vengeance.

A final root of destructive conflict comes when *past experiences in life go unresolved or unexplained.* If we carry into the marriage some hurt from the past, it cannot help but enter into the equation of the relationship.

A husband shares that he becomes anxiety-ridden every time he has the slightest indication that his wife looks at another man. If he sees her talking with another man at church, or if she is gone from the house for too long a time, he finds it almost impossible not to bombard her with questions upon her return home. There is no proof; he only thinks about these things. Their conflicts are growing worse. She says that she cannot live with this kind of accusation every time she has been out of his presence.

When he finally talks with me about his struggle, I ask a question, "Have *you* ever broken trust with your wife or with anyone who was close to you?"

There is a moment of silence as the man takes the question in. Finally with a deep breath he says, "Yes," and he begins to relate the story of a sexual encounter with an old girl friend a few weeks before his marriage to his wife. Then he admits to a brief flirtation with a secretary in their second year of marriage. Little by little he is brought to realize that his accusations against his wife are really accusations against himself. They center on his unresolved and unconfessed infidelity to the covenant between him and his wife. He projects a potential upon her that was actually a reality in himself. When all of this is faced squarely, he kneels and pours out his hidden sin to God. I affirm his forgiveness, and he goes home a few spiritual pounds lighter. The suspicions begin to dissolve, not immediately, for the mental habit patterns must be disciplined. But they do finally disappear.

Unresolved pasts may center not necessarily on personal sins but on painful relationships with parents or close friends. An extremely dominating father may lead a daughter to grow and resent any indications of authority her husband may exert in the home. She may interpret any strenuous attempts on his part to persuade her on matters in which they disagree as a pattern she once saw in her father and against which she rebelled as a child. Not having resolved her hostile parental relationship, she lets it carry over to her husband and takes out on him the rebellious anger she once felt for her father. The conflict becomes destructive.

Here is a place for healing, and the sensitive husband or wife listens to the other talk about the past. When the hint of hurt emerges, they study it together. Has it been resolved? Has the act of another been forgiven? Has the pattern of transferring the blame to someone else been broken? Does the person see his or her spouse as someone entirely different from the one who inflicted the hurt? If the answer to any of these is negative or unsure, you can be certain that it will be a breeding ground for conflict which can destroy. And that means that companionship will be inhibited.

The Weapons of Marital Warfare

Constructive conflict, the kind that would have taken place in the garden before the rebellion of Adam and Eve, is not as rare as we might think. We are conflicting with one another with almost unbroken frequency in a marriage where communication flows freely. That may surprise some, but the point is that we equate conflict so completely with anger that we do not realize that the exchange of ideas in sharing is by definition conflict, but it is constructive conflict.

"Tomorrow is John Becker's birthday," a husband may say to his wife. "We've got to get a card in the mail to him." She responds, "Dear, John is a good friend of yours; surely you're going to send more than a card." Ideas and opinions have differed. There is agreement on the fact of a friend's birthday; there is disagreement about what should be the appropriate observance.

"Honey, I can't go around buying presents for every friend of mine who has a birthday. John doesn't care about gifts like that anyway." Husband has set forth his basic case.

"John Becker simply isn't just another friend; he's probably your best friend. Didn't he take you to a ball game a month ago?"

"Yes, he did."

"Didn't John show you how he feels about you when your father died and he was over here almost constantly every day for a week to see how you were doing?"

"Yes, he did that. But I've shown my thanks for each of those things. I wrote him a note each time saying how much I appreciated what he'd done. You don't go around giving grown men presents every time they have a birthday, though."

"Well, maybe most men don't. But here's your chance to be different. John is turning fifty tomorrow, and it's a chance to pick out something very personal that will express the fact that you know this is an important moment in his life and how much he means to you. Just taking the time to choose something will mean a lot to him. Why don't you do something that he would never expect you to do?"

Husband can bring this discussion to a conclusion in one of three ways:

He can say: "Yeah, I can see what you're saying. It *would* mean a lot to him. What do you suggest that I try to get?" Here, husband has listened to both sides—his and his wife's—and he's decided that her thinking is sounder and more productive than his. So impressed is he that he's going to consult her even further. He'll probably discover that she has a ready answer. (She may have even already bought the gift for her husband to give John Becker.)

Secondly, the husband could conclude the discussion by saying, "Why do you always insist that I think about things like this when I've got a busy day ahead of me? I wouldn't care for a birthday present from John; why would he care that much about one from me? But if it will make you happy, I'll pick something up while I'm getting the wheels balanced on the car." The conflict now ends in a draw. In one sense the wife has won—if winning means that a present for John Becker is going to be purchased and given—but in another sense *no one* has won. Husband's spirit is less than admirable about the whole thing, and he is only going to do this to get his wife off his back. He will do what she suggested, but he is not going to admit that her thinking was superior to his. It will probably make her less inclined to give her opinion the next time. She's probably wondering if it was worth it this time.

A third response: "Now come on! You always come up with dumb ideas like this when someone has a birthday. John Becker isn't a kid anymore; I'll send him a card. Now let's forget it; I don't have time today, and I hate to buy presents. Forget it!" No one looks good on this one. Husband sees his wife's ideas as ridiculous and time-consuming. He really doesn't even want to defend the validity of his own thinking. He escapes the conflict with a sidestep; he simply isn't going to do anything.

The first response was constructive conflict at its best. Husband and wife would both leave the discussion happy: she that her husband was willing to take her counsel and change his mind—he, that his wife was wise enough to help him see a good thing. No one thought of it as conflict, but it was. But the admirable aspect of it was that the discussion centered upon the issue, not the people. No one felt that the results of the discussion were going to be potentially humiliating or swing the balance of dignity away from them. No one had to win.

The second response is half-baked. It cannot be called constructive because no one appears to have learned anything. The wife got her point across, but—at least according to the data we have—husband did not necessarily mature in his insight, nor did he feel that an issue had been well clarified. The conflict was at best simply an exchange; it did not produce a deeper feeling of companionship.

The third response was a loser. And it brings us to the fact that destructive conflict employs a number of weapons which can tear people apart and leave relationships devastated as if in the wake of a hurricane.

Take the weapon of *silence,* for example. Perhaps it sits near the top of the list of common tools of conflict. When the issue becomes sharp between husband and wife, the user of silence simply clams up. He reminds me of the turtle who senses danger and retreats into his shell. He will not respond to his partner's points; he will not identify the issues which have hurt him or improved upon his own position. Mainly, he just boils and fumes within. He makes silence an iron curtain that no one can penetrate. He can literally hold this stance for days, if necessary. With each day the awfulness of this weapon grows as its very use inflates the issue far beyond its original scope.

Silence is most dramatic when a couple crawl into their double bed at night. It is less dramatic if they have twin beds, meaningless if they have separate bedrooms. There they lie, geographically six inches apart. But the silence gives them the emotional sense of being ten miles apart. They almost feel the imaginary spatial distance as they maintain very correct supine positions. No one dares move a leg, arm, or hip toward the middle of the bed, for fear that an accidental touch might signal the resumption of a conversation, or even—horror of all horrors—indicate a desire to apologize and surrender the issue.

At first, silence can be helpful if it stands as a buffer while each partner takes a moment—as if in a declared truce—to sort out his thinking on the disagreeable issue. This is good silence if one is using the time to say, "Does he have a point; could I be wrong?" A second possibility for this brief time of silence would be to think, "I can see that she doesn't understand my position on this one, and it's very important that she learn how I feel. How can I get her to see it without hurting her or making her feel that I've always got to defend my position?"

But if this truce-like silence lasts for very long, it becomes misunderstood. There are times when a partner might wisely say to his companion, "Look, do you mind if I take a few minutes to think about what you've just said? Let me sort it out before I say anything more."

But the "turtle-strategy" and the "truce-strategy" should not be confused. They are two different things altogether. The "turtle" is a clam-up, and the longer he refuses to give the conflict the air it needs, the harder it will be to bring the issue to a constructive conclusion. Finally, the other partner will begin to pull punches on issues because he does not want to face the long periods of silence which invariably come when his spouse turns away and pouts like a child.

Something insidious happens during silence. We foster feelings and opinions in our spirits which begin to build into monstrous thunderclouds. When the cataclysmic explosion finally comes, the war may be atomic in scope while the issue is actually the size of a peanut. But silence has inflated everything.

A second weapon follows on the heels of silence. In fact the use of this weapon often compels a second person to use silence as a defensive maneuver. I call this weapon *word-missiles.* In constructive conflict, good use of words can make the clash a happy experience. Words have to be carefully chosen in a helpful debate. They cannot be inaccurate, fraught with emotional overtones and second meanings, and they must target right on the issue, away from the person. In learning how to trade words properly, some couples have worked very hard to restate exactly what they heard the other person to say before they launch into a response of their own. This way both are sure that the response is based on an accurate understanding of what the first person said. "I heard you say that you are upset because I let the kids go over to their friend's house when in fact you are ready for supper. The fact is, however, that I didn't let them go. They gave me the impression that you had already said it was fine with you."

During the Senate hearings at Watergate, Senator Ervin suggested that everyone take notice of what he called Ervin's law: that in an exchange of words, there are actually three meanings: first, what the speaker thinks he said, secondly, what the listener thinks he heard, and, thirdly, what the actual words meant according to a dictionary. Ervin's law operates with vigor in every marital conflict.

The misuse of words can quickly turn conflict into something destructive. Volatile words which cut the personality can be brought up to the front line when a person feels that he is losing and wants to regain control: "childish, stupid, maniac, frigid, and witch" are a few samples. Verbal overkill can sweep attention away from an issue quite swiftly: "You never . . ." or "You always . . ." are designed to take an isolated situation and generalize it until it appears to have marked the entire marriage of ten or more years.

Verbal A-bombs are those words which when dropped cannot be forgotten long after the issue of conflict is. This is the word-missile of the unrestrained person who cares more for his self-preservation than he does the dignity and self-esteem of his partner. "I'm sick and tired of your *constant* (verbal overkill) complaining. I'm *never* going to satisfy you in a thousand years (small A-bomb). *The worst decision I ever made in my life* was to marry you (big A-bomb); I'd have *been a lot happier without this kind of thing* facing me every day when I get home" (second large A-bomb). For weeks, the wife who hears this will be reminded every time her husband comes through the door of what he has said.

A third weapon of marital warfare comes into play when we employ *deliberate vindictive actions.* Watch this one, for when partners reach this level of destructive performance the conflict has reached an inflammable state. The issue has been eclipsed by the desire to punish. Now we are talking about pure vengeance. Its objective is to humiliate, force unconditional surrender, or gain some twisted satisfaction out of seeing the other person suffer.

One type of vindictive action is the withholding of

certain marital privileges. Among the most frequent is the withholding of the sexual experience. This is a very sensitive issue in a marriage, and if the weapon is employed with regularity it begins to signal the "good boy" idea of sex. If you're a *good boy* today, wifey will allow her *good boy* to make love tonight. But if you're not a *good boy*, well, maybe tomorrow night. In this usage, sex soon becomes a demeaning affair, and both come to hate it for opposite reasons. Wife, because it is only a tool; husband, because it is something to be earned. Soon they come to sexual encounters only to meet instinctive sexual needs, and finally even that gets suppressed or turned off. Sometimes one or both begin to look in another direction.

Other vindictive actions include the sharing of the issue with the children, and, just as bad, letting neighbors and friends in on the grand battle. One subtle way is to bring the issue up among a set of close friends as a prayer request.

Add violence to your list of vindictive actions; it happens more than one realizes. Here again, we're back to the necessity to teach our children restraint of emotions at an early age. Couples prone to massive explosions of temper will lose sight of the issue and begin to throw things (a female tendency) and hit one another (a male tendency). In counseling with young women who are making the decision to say yes to a proposal of marriage, I often ask what they know about their fiances' temper under stress conditions. They often admit that they do not know anything about this. They could not imagine, anyway, that the one they love could ever resort to violence. But the incidence of bruises, black eyes, and swollen muscles I see covered up by makeup in church on Sunday morning leads me to believe that violence occurs in more homes than one might expect.

We have almost reached the bottom of the arsenal of marital warfare when we consider marital infidelity or the threat of it as a possibility. To me the word infidelity implies the physical breaking of the commitment to remain faithful. Unfaithfulness begins when a person storms out the door of the home and leaves. In that one act, he has brought silence, repudiation, and vindictive action all into play. And on top of it he has added the statement, "I quit the relationship at least for now; get along for yourself."

The degree beyond walking out, of course, is the entrance into another relationship. The rebellion against a partner has taken its worst turn if our unfaithfulness carries over into establishing another relational experience, whether it be for a few moments or an indefinite period of time. From a destructive perspective, it is the supreme way of getting back, of hurting another person. But the final tragedy is that the rebellious weapon points in more than one direction, and everyone is generally destroyed.

The memories that infidelity create are almost impossible to erase. Long after there may have been reconciliation, both will wonder if the person who left found something in that fleeting alternative experience that was more appealing. They always wonder what it will take to set off another experience like the first. And so they are not themselves any longer. There is always a kind of fear and insecurity; he or she did it once; will he do it again?

The weapons of marital warfare go from gentle jabs to blows of massive megatonnage. Companionship rests on our ability to use the techniques of conflict wisely and sensitively—building, not destroying; healing, not hurting; sharing, not demanding. There will be conflicts; the question is, what kind?

Final Solutions

Conflict—destructive or constructive—must have an end point to it. Even the best of conflicts become gradually negative in contribution if they are repeated over and over again without a final resolution. That points up the necessity for husbands and wives to be on the alert for recurring themes of disagreement which may demand some sort of summit conference to bring to a conclusion.

David and Lynn never go to a gathering of friends, for example, that they do not come home angry at each other. Lynn physically tires as the evening goes on and usually wishes to leave at an early hour. But David is a "slow starter" in social groupings. He is often silent during the first half of the evening and then gets more conversational as the time goes by. But just about the time that he is warmed to the momentum of the evening, his wife asks him to leave. Inevitably, they go home frustrated after he has asked for at least four different extensions on their moment of exit.

As they leave the party, David is looking over his shoulder at the good time left behind, and Lynn is looking at the privacy of the car where she will no longer have to feel embarrassed over the insensitivity of her husband. In this pressured and fatigued state, they conflict destructively. Arriving home, they go to bed in silence, rise the next morning in grogginess, still saying nothing, and spend a miserable day at their jobs hoping the other will call and break the relational misery. Finally that night, out of sheer emotional exhaustion, the quarrel is smoothed over. No one says anything; they just independently choose not to raise the problem any further.

The trouble is that the issue is not resolved. It is compacted down into the soul, stamped upon to make room for other things, and simply festers until another similar occasion calls it up again. When it surfaces again, the anger will be a bit greater, the hurt a bit deeper.

The answer for David and Lynn is a summit conference, a discussion of this problem when feelings are not running so high. Dave has to be told in some impressive way that his wife is a human being whose physical system simply turns off early in the evening. It is the way she has come to be; she is not happy about it, proud of it, or able to change it. On the other hand, Lynn must come to grips with the fact that her husband is a late-nighter. His individual personality style—which can only be slightly modified—makes him the way he is. When he asks her to stay later, he is not thinking to himself, "How can I hurt Lynn and make her mad?" He is caught up in the tempo of the moment, and he simply doesn't understand.

Either David and Lynn can let this become a pattern for constant friction—as most couples will—or they can attack the problem. So they lay out the issue assuring each other that a solution is necessary and possible. They must immediately go on the assumption that their behavior has never been designed to hurt the other. And this must be *believed* by both if they are to go further. So they begin to agree about future action.

When a later-than-normal evening is anticipated, Lynn will plan her day to get some late afternoon rest. She will schedule herself so that she doesn't have to use this time for anything else. On the way to the gathering, they will agree to leave at a certain time, and that David will initiate the leaving. Lynn will trust David to keep this covenant, and David will hit the target as close as possible. She will not be upset if it is a few minutes beyond the deadline, nor will David deliberately crowd the deadline legalistically if a graceful good-bye can be said a few minutes earlier. Their compromise is based on a mutual trust; leaving later than Lynn would normally have left and leaving earlier than David would normally have chosen. This time when the compromise is implemented and they walk out the door, both are happy with the evening, but even happier that they have jointly solved a previously destructive problem. They respect each other and are therefore happy with each other. The ride home is a satisfying one, and they have developed a form of mature companionship through constructive conflict.

No single person won in this conflict; the relationship won because it was built. This is what I call a presolution to a conflict. A couple discerns a destructive theme, analyzes it outside of the heat it causes, and affirms a plan of action that avoids the fallout the next time around.

But what if there hasn't been a presolution? Is there the possibility of a postsolution? Certainly, and it is the one with which we are most familiar. I cannot think of any better words than to say it is called *confession and forgiveness.*

Conflict has to have a postsolution moment when the war is called to an end. A line must be crossed where both can say, "There no longer exists anything between us; my toe can touch her toe, his arm can touch mine, and the six-inch barrier is broken down."

It is hard to say, "I was wrong; I'm sorry." Going back to that bed scene in which two stiff bodies lie side by side, I wonder how many of us have lain in such a situation and contemplated the difficulty of filling the darkened air with just a few simple words, "Darling, I can see where I'm wrong; forgive me." In the rational moment it appears to be such an easy thing to do, but in the heated moment it calls on every bit of spiritual and mental energy we have.

How very often the walls tumble like Jericho's the minute one makes a statement of confession. Two lovers rush to each other's arms and embrace intensely. What they wanted most from each other has happened; the conflict is resolved.

We have to cultivate the ability to apologize by meditating upon it in advance of those times when it may have to happen. We have to ask God each day for a soft heart to learn when we're wrong and declare it. The man or woman who has learned to confess his wrong does not master that ability on the spot, in the heat of conflict. He learns it first as a child from parents who teach him the value of repentance and confession. He learns it throughout his lifetime, continually praying for the ability to face the facts that show him when he is wrong.

Dr. David Seamands tells of a missionary who was on a trip speaking to American audiences about his overseas ministry. One Saturday morning during an early part of a service in which he was to speak, a note called him off the pulpit to a telephone. It was his wife calling long distance from their home. "One of the boys is giving me trouble," she said. "I need your advice about what to do."

Caught in the preoccupation of his impending message, the missionary snapped at his unsuspecting wife, "Don't you realize I'm about to speak here? You can handle the situation better than I can from this distance; I'll be home in a few days." Saying a terse good-bye he returned to the pulpit and preached.

But the next few hours gave him no inner rest. His wife had had a need; he had crushed her attempt to reach out to him. He was dead wrong and he had to make it right. He would call her that night, he told himself, and have a long talk, solve the problem, and assure her of his love. But he could not settle down with this solution either, so he decided to make the call immediately. They talked for a long time, and he did apologize—pointing out his insensitivity and selfishness. After sharing many endearments, they said good-bye. When the missionary's wife hung up the phone, she decided in her new, happy frame of mind to take a brief bicycle ride before starting supper for the children. Pedaling a few blocks from her home, she crossed an intersection where a drunken driver slammed through a stop sign failing to stop. She was hit and instantly killed.

When Dr. Seamands told the story, he stopped at this point and let the impact of the situation sink into the ears of those who were breathlessly listening. Then he posed the stunning question: "Can you imagine how many times in his grief that missionary was thankful that he had called his wife that afternoon and set straight the record of his sin?"

Gail and I have spent our years in the ministry saying frequent good-byes as I have made trips across the country to speak. More and more we realize that when one flies enormous distances with frequency, any day could be the last of our earthly relationship. I don't know why flying highlights that reality, for they tell me that the drive to the airport is more dangerous than the flight. But these frequent trips do make me face the possibility that each good-bye could be the last. Living with death in the experience of people to whom we minister has further heightened this awareness, and it all causes a general relational discipline between us. We learn never to leave one another for a day—in town or out of town—without resolving any and all conflicts that have need of forgiveness and restoration.

Both of us have spent far too many tragic moments with surviving husbands or wives who have privately confessed that at the time of the spouse's death, the two partners were totally out of touch with each other. He had stomped out of the house in anger; she had let him go in silence. Now there was no time for forgiveness. These are the kinds of agonies that enhance the grief at funerals that people see, but never quite understand.

How ugly the unresolved conflict which begs to be ended through apology. How tragic the apology which is not met with forgiveness. It is absurd to say, "Love is never having to say you're sorry." On the contrary: love is the exact opposite. Love is being able to admit what you are and apologize for it with the expectation that you will be accepted through forgiveness. Love is being able *to say* that you are sorry.

Our marriage relationships can grow only to the limits of our ability to forgive. To forgive is to choose not to raise an issue again for which there has been confession and apology. And in the mutual exercise of apology and forgiveness, there is growth in sharing; the making-up is sheer joy. There is a beautiful peace, for the war is ended.

Companionship
Through
Cooperation

Prudential Insurance suggests that if you purchase one of their policies you can "own a piece of the rock." I would like to suggest that a marriage will never know full companionship—the joining of minds in sharing—until it owns a piece of ministry.

Young couples come to my study to talk about their decision to marry. I have learned to ask a question to which I expect little or no answer. "What is the vision of your marriage?" I ask. The vision? They look at me bewildered, perhaps a bit sorry that they came. I ask the question again, for I wish to make the event of the question as important as the answer. "What is your vision?"

I observe that the girls attempt an answer first most of the time. The answer I most often hear goes something like this, "I guess our vision is to make each other as happy as possible." That is the answer I've come to learn to expect, and the one on which I gleefully leap so that a significant point about God's plan of relationship can be made. "Your vision," I state firmly, "is not good enough."

Now it is the turn of the young man to react. He was beginning to entertain pleasant illusions of his wife making him happy, and now I am suggesting that that isn't good enough. He is sure now that they should not have come. So I follow up my counsel with further clarification.

A marriage which sets as its highest vision or goal the making of each other happy is doomed to mediocrity.

Happiness in marriage is not an end, an objective. It is the *result* of meeting other objectives. The Christian believes that true happiness is found in fulfilling God's plan for one's life. If there is a plan for individuals, there may be reason to believe that there is a kind of plan for a relationship.

Adam and Eve certainly had a plan given to them for their relationship. As long as they pursued that plan, there was apparent happiness. When they stepped outside the boundaries of that plan, their happiness was affected.

I don't read many things in the Bible about the happiness of couples, but I do read of marriages that had a ministry. Reading between the lines, one gets the sure and certain feeling that the couples who performed ministry were indeed very happy with each other. Take Aquila and Priscilla as an example. There is a picture of teamwork: ministry which was bigger than either one of them.

Sarah and Abraham cannot be left out. We read much about Abraham's faith; but don't overlook Sarah's willingness to go along with all of Abraham's decisions. Each made serious mistakes to be sure, but the overall picture is one in which they shared a vision that involved being what God wanted them to be, and providing the conditions in which they could be used to foster the ultimate birth of Israel. I am drawn to Hannah and Elkanah who, when their son, Samuel, was born, brought him to the tabernacle for God's service. It would have been an almost unthinkable challenge had not both of them been convinced that God had something special for them and their son.

I have never been convinced that the will of God has involved his selection of one specific person for each of us to marry. I remember how many times this kind of thinking was foisted upon us when we were young. Somewhere out there—pointing to the horizon somewhere in the direction of Brooklyn—is a lovely girl the

Lord has picked out for you, I was told. Even as a young boy I would find myself brooding over this and wondering what "that girl the Lord had picked" was doing at this very moment.

The logic of that kind of reasoning now escapes me. If we seriously believe that there is only "one best" person in the world for us, what happens if that "one best" makes a bad decision somewhere on the trail to our special meeting? What if she dies in an accident? Am I alone for the rest of my life? Do I infer when I read of an accident which has taken the life of a young man, "Well, there goes somebody's chance to marry?"

I am of the settled opinion now that each of us could probably have married any one of a number of different persons and been happy. He or she would certainly have to be within the parameters of reasonable compatibility, but then we would not have caught up with them if they had not been. Happiness consists not of being married to a special person. Rather, it rests on doing things according to God's design, in obedience to the way he wishes us to act in every opportunity set before us. "Happy are those who keep my ways," the voice of wisdom—God's law of common sense—cries out (Prov. 8:32). "Blessed . . . is the man whose delight is in the law of the Lord . . ." (Ps. 1:1, 2), the Psalmist says. Happiness is doing things right. Happiness in marriage is doing things right together.

The one greatest thing Jesus calls people to be is servants not only of one another, but to the world. And that is what I mean by ministry. What is your ministry? Your relationship will only be as happy as you are willing to combine your talents, resources, and energies, and learn to serve together from the base of your marriage.

Naturally, our ministry to our children would be at the top of the list of people to serve. We are in an age where parents find it expedient to farm out the bringing up of their children to nursery and day care centers, community recreational centers, expanded public school sessions and everything else now available. This bizarre system releases couples for more opportunities to make more money to buy more things, which in turn will create a busier schedule in which the children will experience more separation from their parents.

It would be a certain step toward happiness if a husband and wife were to make the decision that they were going to deliberately restrict their standard of living so that one salary would be adequate for all family needs. Then greater attention and time could be centered in the "ministry" of the family toward its children.

Beyond children, a couple must have a ministry among the fellowship of Christians—preferably in the church. In our church, we encourage couples to work as teams teaching in the church school, working with young people, or heading up our small fellowship groups. We want them to analyze their mutual gifts and employ them together. Too often the church has separated husband and wife—sometimes it has to happen— and denied them a kind of happiness which is their right to have in ministry. If I were a layman, I would insist on a ministry in the church which my wife and I could perform together. Why not husband and wife teams doing the ushering? We often have husbands and their wives give the prayers in our services; one begins the invocation; the other completes it. The same is done at Scripture reading time. In those cases, the event may be more important than anything else, for we are visibly saying, "Here is a husband and wife praising God and leading us together."

This kind of companionship begins when we specifically own a piece of ministry. It means that we've had to sit down and prayerfully discuss together what our goals of service will be. During this past year, Gail and I experienced a burden to get to know the widows and divorcées in our congregation. We planned to invite them one by one to our home for evening meals on an every-other-week basis. We have enjoyed giving special monetary gifts to young couples struggling through school or heading toward missionary service. We are always setting some objective of mutual ministry which we can share together.

Our companionship and happiness grows, not because of the results, but because of the exercise of doing it. If there had never been one result of anything we had done together, the sheer excitement of planning and executing a ministry has been worth it all. We are happy because we have mutually emptied ourselves of something for someone else.

In our mutual ministry, as we commit ourselves to something outside of our relationship, there comes a freedom and desire to praise one another. Gail and I have often been told that our faces shine with radiance when we are watching the other do something in service to God. I sense that Gail seems to be sitting on the edge of her seat, notebook and Bible open when I am preaching. I, in turn, can scarcely contain my joy when I see her sharing with seminary students how to conduct themselves as husbands and fathers in the ministry. We are not competitive because the goal is always before us. Neither of us resents the spotlight well-meaning friends might turn on the other in a moment of thankfulness because we know it all belongs to God, and we are privileged to share it.

Perhaps the authenticity of companionship is most demonstrated at death. If so, J. C. Pollock's description of the death of Hudson Taylor's second wife, Maria, will give unimpeachable evidence as to how close the two of them had become because they were committed to a ministry of missions in China that was bigger than themselves. In the heat of high fever this conversation ensued:

"My hair is so hot!" she said.
"Oh, I will thin it out for you, shall I?" Hudson

knew she did not like her hair cut short because it could not be done nicely in the Chinese way.

Her hair was matted and tangled by sweat. He began to cut it all off except for an inch fuzz.

"Would you like a lock sent to each of the three children? What message shall I send with it?"

"Yes, and tell them to be sure to be kind to dear Miss Blatchley . . . and . . . and . . . to love Jesus."

When he stopped cutting she put a hand to her head.

"That's what you call thinning out?" she smiled. "Well, *I* shall have all the comfort and *you* have all the responsibility as to looks. I never do care what anyone *else* thinks as to my appearance. You know, my darling, I am altogether yours," she said. And she threw her loving arms, so thin, around him and kissed him in her own loving way for it.

Later as the morning drew on, another conversation between Hudson and Maria began:

"My darling, are you conscious that you are dying?" She replied with evident surprise, "Dying? Do you think so? What makes you think so?"

"I can see it, Darling."

"What is making me die?"

"Your strength is giving way."

"Can it be so? I feel no pain, only weakness."

"Yes, you are going Home. You will soon be with Jesus."

"I am sorry . . ."

"You are not sorry to go to be with Jesus?"

"Oh, no!" ("I shall never forget the look she gave me," Hudson later said, "as looking into my eyes she said:")

"It's not that. You know, Darling, that for ten years past there has not been a cloud between me and my Saviour." ("I know that what she said was perfectly true.") "I cannot be sorry to go to Him," she whis-

MAGNIFICENT MARRIAGE

pered. "But it does grieve me to leave you alone at such a time. Yet . . . He will be with you and meet all your need."

"Soon after nine," Pollock writes, "the breathing sank lower. Hudson knelt down. With full heart, one of the watchers wrote, he 'committed her to the Lord; thanking Him for having given her, and for the twelve and a half years of happiness they had had together; thanking Him, too, for taking her to His own blessed Presence, and solemnly declaring himself anew to His service.'"

Hudson Taylor had lost his wife and a baby. Pollock quotes the words of Taylor, "My heart wells up with joy and gratitude for their unutterable bliss, though nigh to breaking. 'Our Jesus hath done all things well.'"[12]

Who of us does not covet the companionship, the sharing of minds, to such a depth that we cleave to mutual transparency. We hunger to reach into another life and explore the unlimited depths of what personhood is. We crave to unburden ourselves of all we are and hope to be. We seek to share in our love. But such companionship is not purchased through pleasurable experiences, the spending of money, and traveling far and wide. It is found in goals and objectives of ministry which expend the two of us beyond our own interest— into the interests of God and his people.

Companionship is communicating, conflicting constructively, and cooperating in ministry. It is one step further on our pilgrimage to becoming one flesh.

SERVICE:
TO SUPPORT

OF ALL THE HUMAN STRUGGLES, LONELINESS seems to be the worst. It is the first human dilemma mentioned in the Bible.

> Then the Lord God said, It is not good for man to be alone . . . (Genesis 2:18).

The significance of that statement grows as it is measured in the rhythmic beat of the author's comment that at the end of every phase of creation, the Lord called each thing "*good.*" "It is good; it is good," God would say. Now we come to something that isn't good, and that is man's aloneness.

Aloneness is not good because our nature is relational. God made us to have relationships. It is in our relationships that we are either built or destroyed. A man and woman meet, and there is a chemistry of relationship following their marriage. A father, commenting on his son three years after the boy's marriage, says, "I never thought he could amount to much, but that little wife of his has brought qualities out of him that I didn't think existed." What the father doesn't realize is that his observation is quite theological. Our relationships change us: they make us something, or they reduce us to nothing.

When Paul met Janelle in college, it didn't take long for romance to begin. The initiative in their attraction seemed to come more from Janelle than from Paul, but then she was twenty-three years of age, while he was twenty-one. Those who knew Janelle were aware that she had come through a number of relationships with men in which engagement seemed imminent—only to end suddenly with little explanation from Janelle, except to say that it wasn't the Lord's will. From the male side, however, the story was that Janelle was hard to get along with, that she was strong-minded, and difficult to deal with when her mind was made up.

Paul was quiet but well liked. His professors all

remarked about his ability to think things through. He was sincere, truthful, and sensitive. If he could develop a bit more force in his personality, he might become an effective pastor. Friends of Paul and Janelle were equally divided on the wisdom of their relationship. Some said Janelle would be good for Paul. She would push him. She would transfuse her strength and forcefulness into him. They felt that if anyone could bring out the best in Paul, Janelle would be the person.

As time went by, however, it gradually became evident that this wasn't going to happen. They married and graduated from school. Over the years they moved from church to church, changes occurring about every twenty-four months. Paul was not performing as an effective pastor. The big question asked more than once was why had Paul failed to live up to his potential?

Could his wife be blamed for Paul's ineffectiveness? Certainly one could not heap all the responsibility upon her. But then it was hard to avoid exploring the meaning of certain remarks. For example, take the comments of a layman who, after sitting under Paul's ministry for eighteen months said, "You could never be quite sure who was the real pastor of the church. The minister and his wife were fine people, but you always had this feeling that she didn't think her husband was sharp enough. In a conversation in which both of them were involved, she had to add or correct something each time he spoke. Sooner or later you would see him go into a shell if she persisted."

Or listen to the observations of a young woman in another church who a few years before had been a frequent babysitter for Paul and Janelle's children. "Pastor and his wife often came home from various church affairs obviously angry at each other. You could sense his quiet hostility toward his wife. As they entered the house, it frequently seemed as if she was criticizing something he'd said or done. He would look defeated and crushed. I remember thinking more than once about how his manner would change when he drove me home. He would suddenly become quite talkative. Now that I am older I recall with some shock that he often drove me home by the longest route and the slowest possible speeds. It dawns on me now that, consciously or unconsciously, he enjoyed talking with me because he knew that I looked up to him and admired him. Frankly, I think in retrospect that he was attracted to me. I kind of met a need in his life that his wife may not have been meeting. Had I been something less than a naive teenager, I wonder if I would have been able to handle the truth of what was really going on in those days."

Perhaps the saddest of all comments comes from one of Paul and Janelle's children many years later: "My mother had a way of never letting up on my father. I think she had an image of what kind of a man she wanted to be married to, and she was going to force Dad into that mold whether he liked it or not. It made her hypercritical of everything he did. He could never please her. She would badger him in front of the kids about matters like why didn't he make the deacons see how badly the parsonage needed remodeling; why didn't he stand up to a certain man or woman; why hadn't he told her about a certain situation brewing in the church? She never let him rest. I can remember some times when Dad would come home exhausted and want Mother just to sit down with him; he would reach out to touch her, and she would jerk back. Even as a kid something told me that to be rejected physically like that must have been terribly painful. Mother just never took the time to find out who Dad was. She was too involved in trying to force him into being what she wanted in a man."

When Paul and Janelle's marriage fell apart, it was assumed that Paul's unfaithfulness to his wife was the cause. Some blamed the woman in the neighborhood with whom he had the adulterous liaison; others blamed him for not appreciating his "godly" wife. If the three comments we have studied are true, however, you may be able to see that long before the incidents of unfaithfulness, relational faults and cracks were growing that made the ultimate destruction of the marriage inevitable. In Paul and Janelle's case, the result was separation and humiliation. In many similar cases, where nothing as dramatic as adultery has taken place, couples continue to live in a kind of neutral coexistence or tense stalemate.

At the root of Paul and Janelle's marriage was the failure of servanthood. The comments tell us more about Janelle than they do about Paul. All three spotlight a woman who was trying to shape a man rather than serve him. She had failed to see that people change and mature not by demand or force of personality. Rather, they grow because someone else has created conditions in which growth can take place.

Paul had been a man of apparent potential; so said those who knew him in earlier years. If they are to be believed, perhaps he could have grown under the right kind of conditions. Janelle chose to create an atmosphere of change through nagging and pushing. She should, however, have become a servant, not a dictator.

In romance, we feel things together; in companionship, we share things together. But in servanthood, we serve one another and bring about the kinds of changes *that God wants.*

If we believe that God has designed each of us to be a certain kind of person with special kinds of gifts, then the ultimate objective of relationships is to provide ministry which can bring people to the performance standards of that divine design. We make a choice therefore in our relationships: do we change one another to something that *we* want? Or do we effect change in accordance *with what God wants?*

We are not what God wants us to be, the Bible says, because we are sinners. From a practical perspective, that means that we are people whose original design has been warped and twisted. We are bundles of secrets, shames, and selfish habits. Until the secrets are revealed, the shames forgiven, and the habits changed, we will be far from God's plan for us.

A relationship can bring about such changes if it is cast in the servanthood mode. This is exactly what Jesus was trying to get across to his disciples near the end of their thirty-month experience together. We read in John 13,

> Jesus, knowing that the Father had given all things into his hands, and that he had come from God and was going to God, rose from supper, laid aside his garments, and girded himself with a towel. Then he poured water into a basin, and began to wash the disciples' feet and to wipe them with the towel with which he was girded (verses 3-5).

The verse cannot be segmented. It is important to note Jesus' sense of identity. He knew the extent of his authority, his origin, his future, and, therefore, his rights. Symbolically, he laid them all aside and in one act summed up everything he had been doing for the disciples for the past two and a half years: he assumed the role of a servant. In effect he said, "This is what I've been doing for you; I want you to repeat the act in your ministry every day as you come into the lives of human beings."

Servanthood was Jesus' method of bringing about change. As a plant grows to bloom in hothouse conditions, so a man can change when exposed to the love of a person committed not to *demanding* change but serving toward change. The disciples never understood this until they were filled with the Holy Spirit. And when they finally grasped it, they in turn changed the world. Servanthood in marriage requires three things which Janelle never had in her marriage with Paul. The first of them was the principle of *surrender*.

Service
Through
Surrender

Every Christian approach to marriage sooner or later arrives at Paul's great series of relational admonitions to the Ephesians in the fifth chapter of his epistle. The specific teaching on the subject of marriage begins many words earlier when he first concerns himself with the unique lifestyle Christians are supposed to possess. He had warned them in Ephesians 4:17 that being members of the body of Christ meant that they had to step away from the accepted way of life which the Gentiles lived. He dealt with many relational problems such as anger, stealing, and exploitation. When he begins chapter five he becomes positive in his teaching: "Be imitators of God, and walk in love, *as Christ loved us . . .*".

Then Paul again launches into the dimensions of Christian lifestyle which followed in the steps of Jesus. It is in this vein that he brings up the subject of mutual surrender in Ephesians 5:18. Christians do not *exploit* one another; they *submit* to one another. That is a universal principle among all Christian relationships: *it is the element of servanthood.* The best way to bring out the best from one another, Paul is saying, is to serve one another.

Then he sharpens the principle and brings it into the arena of marriage, "Wives, serve your husbands." He probably felt a need to say this because in their new-found faith, the Christian women were taking all kinds of liberties they did not have when they were non-Christians. Women in the pagan world had been play-things, sex-objects, housekeepers, little else. In the fellowship of the Christian church they felt free and began to revel in a new kind of independence which they took to an immature extreme.

Paul goes on to illustrate the dynamics of this relationship. The husband is the head of the wife, he observes, in the same way that Christ is the head of the church, his body, and is himself its Savior. I see the role of Christ in that statement in two dimensions: Christ is *initiator* of relationship as the church's Savior, and he is the *provider* of the relationship in the sense that the church is his body. Later in the paragraph, Paul reveals what he had in mind here when he says in verse 29: "A man . . . *nourishes* and *cherishes* his body as Christ does the church."

In these two general ways a man is head of his wife. He is the initiator of the relationship; in the normal course of things it is the man who asks a woman to be partner with him in marriage. Second, he is normally responsible for nourishing and cherishing his wife, meaning that he provides for her protection, security, health, and welfare. He provides, in other words, for her betterment and growth.

A wife's desire to serve her husband is one of the greatest testimonies to her faith in Christ as Lord. This question of submission has been and will continue to be for some time a focus of controversy as we deal with the question of male and female relationships in the church. There are several facets of this which all of us ought to consider.

First, Paul appears to be recognizing certain offices in the family, just as he did in the previous chapter when he talked about offices in the church which were sovereign gifts of Christ. In the church, these offices provided structure to the body, nurture, and protection. I think Paul's teaching is perfectly consistent here. He casts the husband in the role of head of the marriage relationship, as the one from whom the relationship emanates and the one who will provide the protective perimeter for the relationship in the home.

A second important observation flows from the first. Paul does not imply that headship is domination in the sense of power, and this seems to be where many people misunderstand him. Paul saw offices in the church as authoritative offices and asked people to submit to the men in those offices because it would be a sign of their love for Christ. But these were not *power* positions; rather they were *provision* positions. If the people in the church would submit to the pastor-teacher, he would—under God's direction—provide conditions in which all would grow.

When my wife and I enter our automobile, only one of us can drive. If I am the driver, I am the office holder in that particular relationship. Obviously she is in tacit agreement not to grab the wheel should she have a sudden whim to make a turn or pull over to stop at some store she sees. I, in turn, do not take my position as driver as one of power; rather, as one of providing the means by which we can both safely reach our destination.

One of the things which a person accepts if he submits to the God of the Bible is God's sovereign right to put certain people into certain positions which he chooses. Abraham did not take a civil service exam to compete for the patriarchal role he was given. Nor did Elijah ask to be a prophet any more than Paul submitted an application for apostleship. Throughout the Scriptures God chose men and women for certain functions and opportunities. He made no explanation for his choice except to say that he sovereignly made the choice.

God's choice in the family is for the husband to be the head of the wife. When Paul reaches for historical precedent on this matter, he takes the Corinthians back to the Garden and reminds them that the man was the first human being, and that out of him came a woman. There is a prominence only of order, not necessarily privilege. He goes on to say to the Corinthians, "In the Lord man is not independent of woman, nor she independent of him. . . ." To settle the score he also observes that while the first person was a man, man has been born of woman ever since. For Paul that evens things.

The Genesis account of God's judgment on the first couple is interesting. God turns to Eve, and he pronounces punishment. He does not specifically say what it was that she did; he merely tells her what the future is going to be like. She shall be caught in the paradox of bearing children in deep sorrow, yet at the same time she will be filled with a compelling desire to enter into affectionate relationships with her husband, which in turn will bring about the possibility of more pain. His final statement is, "He shall rule over you."

This is important, not because it is the first time the order of relationships is stated, but because it is restated. In the pre-fall Garden experience, she had been a *helper;* now she is a *subject.* If one looks back to the reason for this, he may want to scan the method Eve used to make her decision about sin in the first place. Her evaluation of the serpent's temptation was threefold: she saw that the tree was good for food (appetite), a delight to the eyes (beauty), and it made one wise (intellect). She made a bad decision, and God relieved her of the decision-making responsibility from then on.

Adam's judgment, on the other hand, does begin with a specific indictment. "Because you did not listen to my voice . . ." God says. Indeed, that is exactly what Adam did not do. He listened to the wrong voice: his wife's, who in turn had betrayed her role as *helper* and brought to Adam a decision founded on slippery ground. Adam had heard the voice of God in Genesis 2:17 before Eve was created. That was the voice to which *he* was to be subject. But he listened to his wife's voice speaking about something she knew nothing about. She had not heard the voice of God; she was ill-equipped to take leadership, but Adam caved in and listened to her anyway. Having listened to the wrong voice, Adam was now going to have to face a creation disturbed and convulsed by sin.

Paul's view of Christian marriage relationship is an attempt to reasonably recover the original Garden situation. It starts with the basics: we are safest when woman deliberately assumes the role of submission. I want to reemphasize that I am not suggesting anything that is not consistent with the order of relationships implicit in the doctrine of the church and, for that matter, in any divinely instituted community in both the Old and New Testament. God sovereignly chooses leaders, and a mark of our submission to God is our submission to those he has placed in leadership over us. The woman who begins her approach to marriage with the principle of submission as a helper firmly in her heart and mind can then begin to provide supportive leadership when it is sought by her husband.

This last thought is worth restating. What Paul is doing is stating the extreme realities of our relationships. This is the honest attitude of the Christian woman who recognizes that her weakness may consist in not always listening to the voice of God. By assuming the role of being subject to her husband, she is identifying with the specific sin of Eve and placing herself in a relational position so that she will not repeat that sin and betray her husband as Eve did hers.

There is a sense here of a theological reality which Western Christians may find it hard to swallow. It is the sense of mutual guilt: we pay for the sins of others, for we are mutually responsible for what each other has done. Woman is paying for the sin of Eve and lives under the headship of her husband: from helper to subject. Husbands are paying for the sin of Adam, having to work in a rebellious creation which is so resistant that it is difficult to enjoy it.

The recreated woman in Christ begins by assuming the role of servant and, by growing in the graces of Christ, becomes the helper once again to her husband.

Now Paul does not stop at theologizing about woman's role. He moves on to the position of the Christian husband. Husbands *love* your wives . . . (how?) . . . as Christ loved the church . . . ." At a first glance, many husbands have thought they have the upper hand in this relationship. Their first mistake is in their misunderstanding of the word *love*. They have equated Paul's view of love with Hollywood's, and thus they have made a fatal mistake.

Remember that when Paul wrote this, he knew nothing of the kind of dating game we play today; he was not thinking of wedding anniversaries, presents, dinners out, red roses, or anything that we think of under the word *love*. For him the word "love" was an action verb, not necessarily packed with romantic feeling. It was a word which spoke of total servanthood. If anyone was in doubt about the kind of servanthood he had in mind, he pointed them to the perfect model of love: Jesus Christ. How did Jesus Christ love the church? Paul responds with a three-point outline. He gave himself for it; he sanctified it; and he will present it in its perfected form, the result of his perfecting work.

This was not the first time Paul seized upon this model to bring people to an understanding of love. To the Philippians he had made the suggestion that Christian relationships were to have the characteristics of Christ's incarnation. Philippians 2:5ff. describes Jesus as surrendering his rights as part of the Godhead, submitting himself to the form and image of a servant, and, being discovered in *that form*, allowing himself to be crucified.

This is the drama of the role Paul has in mind for a man. Again let me point out the doctrine of extremes here that Paul is developing. Paul does not expect a husband literally to die for his wife any more than he expects a woman to be a total slave to her husband. But he has to say this to the Ephesians: you men have not treated your wives with the kind of value in mind that God wants you to have.

This is a practical point to meditate upon for a moment. If a man in his most humble heart-attitude says to himself, I am willing to die for my wife, he will treat her with a reverent tenderness and consideration. It is almost irrelevant to illustrate the point by suggesting the picture of an owner of an expensive automobile. If he has paid an exorbitant amount of money for his car, he is careful to polish it, maintain it, and drive it in conditions in which it will not be damaged or abused. In short, you will find no Rolls Royces on the jeep trails of the Rocky Mountains.

In the same way, when a man looks upon his wife and assumes the inner perspective that he has initiated this relationship at the cost of his own blood, she becomes a valuable associate to him. He will not exploit her, nor will he expose her to degrading conditions.

To give himself for her has some implications of the original meaning of the marriage vow. As Christ gave himself on the cross in total commitment to the church which he loves, so a man gives himself totally to his wife. If what I've said is true, this man will never become a tyrant or a harsh dictator, but he will carefully cultivate his wife's welfare and draw from her the full value of what she has to offer him in the way of precious companionship.

The second thing Paul says that Christ did for the church was to sanctify it. To sanctify is to cleanse, to improve, to set apart for special ceremonial purposes. Theologically, we realize that that is exactly what Christ did for the church. He sanctified the church by washing it with his blood and by giving to it the new direction of the gospel. The church is being sanctified, perfected.

Paul says that a husband is to follow the loving model of Jesus. This means that to love one's wife means to provide opportunities for her to become sanctified, to grow in her experience as a human being toward her God-given potential. I see here the pastoral role of a husband, guaranteeing the spiritual experience of his family. The measurement of such a principle in our families is the answer to this question: is your wife a more mature child of God because she is married to you? Or has your lifestyle and spirit tended to draw her away from her relationship to Christ? The second answer is devastating!

The third principle of husband-love is that of presenting the church to the Father. One senses here the picture of Jesus Christ at the end of the age introducing the church formally to his Heavenly Father. Here is the church, Father, for which I have died, filled with my Spirit, and prayed for in my intercession ministry through the years. Our only conceivable image is a twofold one: the face of the proud groom at a wedding escorting his beautiful bride away from the marriage altar. But see the same man twenty-five years later, the marks of life etched upon his face and body. But his face is even more radiant as he stands for a 25th anniversary portrait surrounded by the family for which he has given so much.

So Christ stands before the Father and says in effect, the church is my most prized possession. I have given myself for it; I have cleansed it; and now it is worthy to be my bride, my highest achievement. I am blessed with the fact that the beauties of the universe are not enough to entice the eyes of the Savior. What he deems most attractive is the sanctified church.

What is Paul saying? That for a man, the greatest achievement and the most prized possession is a wife whom he has loved and served. Briefly, in case anyone has missed his communication, Paul launches into a second allegory to express a man's commitment to his wife. He asks men to reflect upon their care for their bodies. A man who is wise cares for his body. He feeds it, clothes it with protective coverings, and he exercises it. He doesn't exploit it or unnecessarily expose it to situations which will be dangerous for it. Need there be anything else said about what Paul is trying to tell the Ephesian men?

The apostle closes off his teaching on this subject by saying in verse 30, "We do this because we are members of his body." Our submission to one another is a basic testimony to our submission to him. This is very important for young couples to ponder.

Now what Paul has done in this teaching to the Ephesians is to draw a circle of basic human equality. Wives, be subject—husbands, love. While we can see two different points of departure, sovereignly chosen, we see the same basic responsibility on both parts. Both have functions of servanthood: to bring out the best for the other. But it begins with submission, one to the other.

Perhaps a way to illustrate it would be to suggest that a man in the marriage relationship parallels the brain in a human mechanism. The brain is basically the initiator of all actions which the person carries on. But in the healthy situation, the brain does not unnecessarily exploit that initiating privilege. It has learned to work in concert with all other parts of the body—for example, the heart. If the heart begins to beat faster and faster, because the blood flow demands greater pumping power, it may send a message to the brain suggesting a slowdown of whatever function is causing the blood to need to run so swiftly. The brain has learned to trust the judgment of the heart. It processes the judgment of the heart and issues orders to other limbs to cease doing what they are doing. To apply our ridiculous illustration, the brain has submitted itself to the judgment of the heart.

The Ephesian husband, who is by God's choice the head of his home, learns that leadership sometimes means submitting himself to his wife's judgment. Thus a full circle of relationship has been completed, each able to complement the other in his or her weakness. The dynamic of it all is a mystery, and that it can even work is a miracle of God. It is also a paradox for which the world has no answer: the more we serve one another because we are submissive the faster we grow and experience personal freedom to be what God has designed us to be.

Service
Through
Sensitivity

On a trip to Japan I was invited to take a walk through some of the beautiful Japanese forests. All around I noticed men who were at work thinning out the underbrush of the forest. This was a key to the rich growth of trees in Japan. The Japanese have learned to cultivate their forests, reducing those things which were a deterrent to the growth of the tall and healthy trees. Underbrush needlessly consumes nutrients which the soil could better give to trees. Thin the useless vegetation out and cause the important things to grow.

I have learned something from the Japanese about servanthood. Someone has said, "Love is giving someone else a bit of room to grow." Servanthood-oriented husbands and wives are like that. They thin out of their lives and their relationship those attitudes, activities, and abrasive qualities which drain off the richness of the relationship.

If I were to try to cultivate those Japanese forests, I would do more harm than good. For it takes a practiced and sensitive eye to know what needs to be thinned out and what needs to be left behind. My hacking away would be destructive; their manicure of the forest floor is constructive, for they know what to look for. They are sensitive.

If servanthood requires submission, it demands sensitivity. The two great questions in a sensitivity-oriented relationship are these: what are my spouse's *needs* and what are my spouse's *potentials*? *Needs* tend to be the deficiencies of personality and ability which one brings into a marriage and which a partner can help correct. *Potential* describes qualities which can emerge in a person if he or she is encouraged and assisted. Let's talk first about *needs*.

When Christ loved the church, Paul says, he accepted

it as it was. He gave it the gifts of personalities and doctrines that would help it grow. This resulted in a spiritual strength that stopped it from being tossed "to and fro upon every wind and wave of doctrine and the whims of man" (Eph. 4:13ff.).

In marriage, human beings have very definite needs. We discover these needs only as we sensitize ourselves to the human spirit of our spouse. Strange as it may seem, we do not always know our own needs. It often takes a loving relationship to reveal them and do something about them.

One area of potential need often results from the scars and aches of the past. A wife is extremely touchy about being criticized, and when any shortcoming is pointed up to her she dissolves in tears. Her husband is extremely frustrated: he knows that he cannot go through life withholding from her every opinion he has which seems to threaten her self-esteem and personal security. He can choose to punish her on this matter, making her more miserable than ever, or he can begin to ask himself about the past. What has made her so super-sensitive?

Searching conversation reveals a difficult relationship with a father who was never happy with her accomplishments. As a child she had walked on tiptoe for fear that she would feel the harshness of his disapproval. Husband and wife begin to face this fact of the past together. Little by little he is able to show her that his necessary expressions of criticism are not in the same pattern of her unappreciative father. Rather, his comments are designed to make their relationship fuller and more helpful to both. We seldom look back over the shoulder of our spouses and see some of the hurts they have brought with them.

Sensitivity also leads us to make a loving evaluation of the honest weaknesses each has. Some of these weaknesses can be improved upon; others may simply have to be accepted and built around. A certain man entering

into marriage proves to be quite undependable when he
commits himself to a schedule. He is invariably late to
social engagements. It's not that he intends to be dis-
courteous, but he has never fully grappled with the
realities of time. More and more he becomes an irritation to his friends who are always delayed by his
tardiness. His new wife is sensitive to the fact that this is
not a deliberate but rather an unconscious weakness on
his part. She will serve him as she sensitizes herself to
this fact about him. Little by little she sets a higher
standard for his schedule-making. She points up to him
his commitments and highlights the need to get under-
way in advance of the meeting time. She cajoles, she
plans, she affirms him when the pattern begins to
change. She explains to him that she is proud of him,
that she respects him, and that she wants others to love
him as she does. This, in part, will happen if he will
overcome this blind spot. He accepts her desire to make
him into something better through this effort, and the
habit pattern is dissolved and replaced by another more
acceptable one.

We must also be sensitive to the needs caused by
spiritual struggles. We cannot all grow to be mature
Christians overnight, but, on the other hand, none of us
will grow at all in our relationships with God if there is
not someone by us who prods us and pushes us along.
This is part of the pastoral role which was earlier
mentioned in this chapter. As we grow in our marriages
we learn to sense when our spouse is in or out of touch
with the lordship of Jesus Christ. A gentle word, a loving
rebuke in a trusting relationship may be all that is
needed to point out to the other that the heart is a bit
cold today.

It is the lack of sensitivity that is so tragic. The failure
to see the signals of need that hurt so many relationships. Take a typical scene that could have happened in
a million Christian homes just last evening.

When Tom came home from work last night, he was a

combination of exhaustion and frustration. Several things had gone wrong on the job during the day due to a breakdown in company communications and the sloppiness of employees who hadn't done their jobs thoroughly. At home, Tom's wife, Helene, was climaxing an afternoon of domestic disaster. Her eleven-year-old had arrived home from school to announce that mother would have to drop everything and drive downtown to purchase him a special gym suit the school said was absolutely necessary for the next morning. The fourteen-year-old was following Helene around the house nagging for permission to attend a weekend party at the home of people whom neither Tom nor Helene knew. Add to Helene's struggles a dog which was sick and vomiting on the rug, some meat scheduled for supper that refused to become unthawed, a balky vacuum cleaner, and you have a countdown to catastrophe.

It is into that matrix of personal experiences that Tom walks through the door of their home.

Tom: (entering) Boy, am I glad to get home (exchange of perfunctory kisses . . . on the cheek).

Helene: Well, you may not like what you find here.

Tom: Why, hasn't it been a good day?

Helene: It's been awful. First the dog got sick and then the phone rang off the hook . . . and . . . Tom, Tom, where are you? Where did you go?

Tom: (from another room) I'm looking at the paper.

Helene: Oh, no you don't! You have got plenty to handle before you sit down. You're going to have to talk to your daughter; the vacuum is sitting down the hall waiting for you; and I need you to look at the dog—she's sick.

Tom: Look, will you let me relax for just a few minutes? I'm tired of always having one more thing to do.

Helene: Tom, I've been waiting for you to get home. I can't do all of these things by myself. You're simply going to have to . . .

Tom: Now look: I've been looking forward to this quiet time all afternoon. Just a minute of peace is all I want. I haven't been home for four minutes, and you're on my back about things to do. This is *home*, Helene, *home!*

   I put nine solid hours in at the office today so that I could put three meals on the table here. I had a rotten day! Can you please let me rest.

Helene: Now *you* listen! You're not the only one who had it rough. I'm sick and tired of you going off each day and thinking that when you come home you are the only one who's entitled to an easy chair and a paper. Just because you have all those secretaries and assistants thinking you're so great and fawning all over you is no sign that you're going to get the same treatment here.

Tom: I'm not waited on at the office, and I don't want to be waited on here. I only want peace for a few minutes.

Helene: And that's exactly what I was hoping to have too.

There is nothing unique about Tom and Helene's home. They are both victims of events external to themselves. At home, the kids, the dog, and various machines have conspired to upset the balance of harmony. Tom hasn't fared any better at the office. The world which Helene in her anger thinks must be so great has caved in on Tom. What each needed last night was an ally. They both had the same adversity and the same needs, and that is grounds for servanthood. But they weren't sensitive to the fact that they shared such ground.

Tom felt that the best way to solve his problems was to relax, to isolate himself and ignore others. Helene, on the other hand, wanted to face her frustrations by demanding every available hand to spring to her aid. Tom desires inactivity; Helene wants immediate results. Similar needs but dissimilar solutions.

What we are seeing is the beginning of a silent and tense evening. Both will continue taking out on each other the hurt and anger they feel for everyone else. Potential lovers have become, for the moment, real enemies.

What if Tom had come home prepared to talk, and Helene had resolved that despite the panic conditions at home, she would take a ten-minute breather when her husband arrived? What if each one had begun the evening assuming that the other probably had hurts and problems that ought to surface? Suppose that both were sensitive—that at the first exchange of words they had realized that the day had gone wrong for both. They could have walked arm in arm through the house laughing at the chain of disasters, and then they could have gone out for a pizza. But they didn't, and servanthood went sour; the marital friendship collapsed for the moment.

Servanthood in marriage depends upon people who are sensitized to each other's needs. The second area that demands sensitivity is that of each other's *gifts and potentials.* The old prospector's saying, "There's gold in them thar hills . . ." ought to be applied to marriage partners. For each of us is a human bundle of latent talents and gifts which God has created to be used in the fullness of life and service for others. In many cases, the gifts and potentials of people are not uncovered in the marriage experience; rather, they are squelched and quenched. That happens because the love in the home is not servant-oriented. If, on the other hand, a husband and wife pledge themselves to bringing out the best in each other, the "gold" will quickly emerge from what might have been a rather uninteresting human terrain.

Gifts and potentials are first brought out when a marriage partner sets out on a deliberate mission of discovery in the life of the other. For many years my wife was content to sit quietly and listen to me speak to groups in various settings. I often saw, however, that when she visited with people afterwards, it was not long before a larger group would join the conversation she was leading. It was obvious to me that when she said something, people were compelled to listen. I also saw that as our children grew older, they would need her less and she would have to have something that would give her new challenges to develop her personal ministry in the future.

I began to sense that she had a gift of speaking to groups, and to enforce my conclusion, I arranged some situations in which she could test her ability. The results were remarkable. A Sunday school class of women was a success; a woman's retreat at which she spoke was a joy for everyone. When possible I sat down with her and shared some of the methods I had developed for study, note-taking, and preparation. I taught her how to balance a presentation, punctuate it with illustrative material, and then bring people to a conclusion in their thinking. When I came across stories and quotes which I thought might be helpful, I brought home copies for her notebooks. Today her speaking ministry is growing significantly and God is using her because I launched out on a discovery mission to see what was possible in her life.

Suppose that I had resisted the impulse to discover. Perhaps it could have been one of those times when my pride would have made me uneasy about someone in my own home who might become competitive. A part of many of us—not according to God's design—would resist discovery in our partners; it is too possible that they might get the spotlight and attention that we wish to bring upon ourselves.

It is not enough to serve through discovery; there must also be encouragement. I could not have helped Gail that much if I had only made a few remarks about my beliefs in her gifts and potential. I had to encourage, almost push her. She was convinced that this was not something for her, but I felt differently. So I gently affirmed her on many occasions. I pointed out on numerous occasions how people in the groups we visited were attracted to her and what she had to say. I have to confess that on some occasions I even deliberately put her on the spot so that she had to talk to a group and discover her own potential for herself in the moment of performance.

On a smaller scale, Gail had done the same thing for me when we were first married. Education bills kept us poor the first few years, and when something went wrong with the car, it was a major fiscal crisis. One day the brakes went out; they needed to be relined. Now my knowledge of brakes begins and ends with the middle pedal on the floor under the steering wheel. But Gail launched a campaign of encouragement.

"I'm positive," Gail said, "that with your mind you could figure out how new brakes are put on a car." This was insanity, I thought!

"That's not my bag," I responded. "I wasn't taught to be mechanical, and nothing ever works right for me."

Apparently Gail didn't hear my words or she chose—as she sometimes does—not to listen. "I figure that if I stick with you and watch what you do, we can do it together. Let's try it Saturday morning."

Intimidated, even frightened by this pending vehicular surgery, I nevertheless gave in. We bought the parts the salesman said were necessary, collected the tools, and went to work. Gail sat by my side in the driveway with a pad and pencil. As I took things out, she noted the order in which they came, the direction in which they turned, and the way they should look when we would be through. When everything had come out, we simply reversed the order of actions and put all the parts back together again. In four hours the job was done. Then she had the unmitigated nerve to say, "You see, I knew you could do it all the time; next time we overhaul the engine."

It was the same the first time I decided to build a piece of furniture, and it was the same the first time I tried to write an article for a magazine, and it was the same the first time I tried to change the diapers on our first child. Gail, always encouraging—convinced that I could do something I was personally in doubt about. Discover and encourage: the two go together and bring the gold out of an otherwise dry hole.

The other two rules for developing gifts and potentials are *assist* and *release.* Assistance in the case of Gail's speaking ministry came when I helped her develop her abilities to speak and to gather materials that would be helpful to her. We often discussed concepts she was trying to develop and traded ideas about the best way for them to be put across. When I saw that she was serious about testing God's gift in her life, I set her up with a filing system and showed her how to use it. When she asked for it, I gave criticism about how I thought she could do a better job. And so her gift grew.

But it would still have remained useless if I had not been also willing to *release* her. And this is the critical point at which many servanthood opportunities die. For me to release Gail for ministry meant that there were times when I had to stay home while she went out to speak. She had been careful to limit the occasions, but I have been more than willing to man the homefront for an evening—even a weekend on occasion—while she went out to serve the Lord in speaking. It has been a special chance for the children and me to be together and pray for Mother. They have learned that I regard her ministry to be as important as mine, and so they pray for her also.

Many husbands and wives do not release each other to the gifts and potentials God has implanted. They sense a threat to all of it, that it might deny them time or that it might tend to make them less important. A wife resents her husband's acceptance of a Sunday school class because it will take preparation time. A husband berates his wife for the time she spends learning to paint, and in both cases, the dreams of creativity and service are dashed. To release one another means to provide opportunity in which the other can become more of what God wants him or her to be.

I read the dynamic of *release* into the story of Aquila and Priscilla the day they must first have listened to Apollos preach. Together they saw the potential in Apollos as he unfolded his understanding of God. But they also realized that the young man needed some training. One can imagine Aquila taking an offering envelope from the pew-rack and suggesting to his wife in a note that they invite the preacher home for lunch. One can also perceive Priscilla trying to figure out how to make the meat stretch in one more direction. But sensing that there is something important in all of this, she agrees, and the result is a young man schooled and disciplined in the home of Aquila and Priscilla, a couple who released each other to the ministry of hospitality and service. Everyone who came to their home— including the Apostle Paul—was refreshed. Here is a home where servanthood worked.

In his book *I Married You* Walter Trobisch describes a post-evening-service visit to the home of the pastor of the host church where he was speaking in special meetings. He describes the elaborate preparations the pastor's wife, Esther, an African woman, has made to make the remainder of the evening a delightful one. The table is bedecked with steaming food, carefully prepared. One thing is missing: the pastor, who is outside talking with people in the street who wished to visit with him. Trobisch and Esther wait inside, the food growing cold. Esther is embarrassed and frustrated, and Walter seeks to comfort her.

"You suffer," Walter says, "because you are embarrassed because of me."

"I love Daniel very much," she said, "but he is not a man of schedule. I don't mind hard work, but I want to plan my day and have order in my duties. He is a man who acts out of the spur of the moment. He is an excellent pastor. People like him very much. But I'm afraid they take advantage of him, too."

"Your gifts are different, but they could be used to complement and complete each other," Walter responds.

"Maybe so, but we don't know how to coordinate our gifts. We don't throw the balls into each other's hands. We throw them in two different directions. They fall on the ground. No one to pick them up."[13]

"No one to pick them up. . . ." Here is a home with vast gifts and potential, but no apparent servanthood. Two people going in different routes to do their own thing. How unlike Aquila and Priscilla. When the pastor and his wife make the great discovery of sensitivity, servanthood will ignite a love which will make them grow in a way they never thought possible.

Service Through "Serveability"

But servanthood cannot happen if someone is unwilling to be served. And as it is often short-circuited by a spouse who will not assist and release, it is also frequently killed by a partner who will not allow himself to be served.

Peter is a good example. When Jesus began the rounds of the disciples, washing their feet, it was Peter who stepped back in horror. There is no way, Lord, that you are going to wash my feet, Peter said. For Peter it seemed the only thing to do. First, he didn't want Jesus to demean himself like that. Then too, Peter felt a bit embarrassed; why hadn't he thought of that? Add to that a touch of pride: the one whom Peter followed should not have to do such a thing. And in so thinking, Peter completely lost the message that Jesus had been trying to teach for three years.

The ministry of servanthood in the church demands not only servants, but people willing to be served. That's what Jesus meant when he said to him, "Peter, if you will not let me wash your feet, you'll have no part in me."

It was Jesus' way of saying: there is only one way that you can experience the fullness of relationship with me, and that is as you let me enter your life as a servant.

Here is a significant factor that has to be reckoned with in Christian marriage. Are you and I *willing* to be served? Peter thought he was unserveable. But Jesus penetrates that thinking by suggesting that the only way people can be changed is through being vulnerable to service. *Vulnerability* means that we have to let each other into our lives. How?

Vulnerability begins when husbands and wives become free to share and open up their weaknesses to one another. It is one thing for my wife to find weaknesses within me; it is another when I sense the freedom to tell her what I think my inner struggles are. And I have not always found that easy to do, for to share a weakness is one way of putting yourself on the line as wanting change. And I don't always want to change.

A few years ago I began to admit to myself that it was difficult for me to rise early in the morning for a time of personal contact with God. It was hard at first to confess that I would rather sleep than pray. It was even more difficult to admit it to my wife. I became "serveable," however, when I finally summoned the nerve to talk about my weakness. "I want to share this with you," I said, "so that you'll help me. I need you to make sure I've set the clock at night, and that I'll respond to it when it rings in the morning. I'd like you to kick me out of bed if I appear to be ignoring the clock." Gail promised she would, and she did. A weakness I could not handle myself was overcome by allowing Gail to enter into my life and serve me—even if she was rather ruthless about it at times.

Vulnerability comes not only when we share weaknesses, but when we open ourselves to trustworthy criticism from one another. I use the adjective trustworthy because one has to grow in his or her confidence that what a spouse says about our behavior at a party, about our physical appearance, or about the quality of a job we are doing is an accurate appraisal of how things are. But servanthood implies that criticism is given in love, and that it is designed only to build and improve—never to wound or destroy.

Gail and I learned quickly in our marriage that there are times to criticize and times to remain silent. She discovered that the drive home from church was not the time to take my sermon apart. I was too emotionally involved with it to be objective. I learned that the days just before a menstrual period were not the proper time to comment about the taste of a certain vegetable. Better to wait for the moment when there was optimum hunger for improvement and growth.

I am "serveable" when I begin to share my dreams and visions about the future, and I bring my spouse into the stardust of my thinking. I do this now, because little by little my servanthood-oriented spouse has learned that there are conversations stamped "dream." While one might constructively criticize specific plans, one does not trample on dreams. Dreams are not open to editing or ridicule. They are the happy moments in marriage when our wildest thoughts are allowed to soar.

We share them together, and from them a destiny is compiled. We are "serveable" when we release our dreams, and we serve when we do not puncture them. What an ecstatic moment when you discover one other person in the world with whom you can be transparent, who will not shoot holes in your beautiful balloon.

How do we build vulnerability in a marriage? This is a very important question. A wife complains that her husband shares very little with her, that he is a closed book and that she never knows what he is thinking. The husband responds with several episodes in which he had tried to talk about something he felt very deeply only to be met with a Niagara of criticism. "I *knew* all the answers," he says. "I didn't need answers from her; what I did need was someone to sense why I was struggling; she never seemed aware of that." Finally, he stopped trying to find understanding from her, and he turned inward. Here is a couple that needs to build an atmosphere of vulnerability or serveability.

We lay the foundation for vulnerability when we establish in our marriage that acts in the past and facts in the present will not necessarily be held against us in the future. If a man frankly shares with his wife that on a recent business trip he had an inner battle with lust, will she remind him of this every time he goes away in the future? Will it become a theme of criticism to which she returns frequently? Does she allow the sharing to fester in her heart so that her trust in him crumbles?

We are talking about a brand of forgiveness. To establish serveability in marriage is to come to the point where we choose not to hold the past up to our spouse in the future. For a wife who has been betrayed by her husband in the past, this is an extremely difficult spiritual exercise. But she can never hope to regain the lost ground in their relationship until she disciplines herself to do it joyfully.

Serveability grows when we learn the exercise of being able to pray with each other and for each other. Over the years I have been plagued with an occasional series of headaches which come for a few weeks and then go away. On one occasion not long ago when the pain was seemingly unbearable, I asked my wife to lay her hands on me and pray. I remember it as one of the precious moments of our marriage. I had in that act admitted that I was at the bottom of my experience: I was without strength, and I needed her intercession. I would not trade the pain away for anything because through it I have learned the joy there is in asking each other for prayer and knowing that the promised intercession will be there.

Serveability grows a third time when a couple learns that their life together is a shared ministry and vision. As long as two people see their lives as two separate thrusts of existence where they rise or fall on their own merits, there is no marital ball game of consequence. Listen to a married woman who illustrates what I mean:

> Dear Abby: My husband and I do not get along very well. In fact, if it weren't for the kids I wouldn't live within a thousand miles of this idiot. We are both artists and my husband specializes in Western art now, and he has been selling his paintings before the oil is dry on the canvas. I don't mean to put him down, but my work is much better even if it doesn't sell half as well. The public just happens to be going for gimmick art.
>
> I can hardly stand it when my husband sells a painting. For one thing he has a way of gloating that makes me want to put my fist right through his face. I wish I knew how to get over this envious attitude. Can you help me?[14]

No one is serveable in that home because the lifestyle is not shared. It is competitive, not complementary.

In contrast, I think of an elder in our church who enjoys an excellent job in the industrial world as an engineer. His wife has a superior singing voice and is gifted in choral conducting. I have watched him while he quietly sits in the congregation as his wife directs a fifty-voice choir. He delights in sitting with their children while she stands in the spotlight. On choir practice night, he is at home making sure that the children have a continuity of parental fellowship while their mother is gone. I sense that every time she lifts her arms for the downbeat, his heart is in tune with hers. Her musical performance to the glory of God is not hers alone; it belongs to them both. It is *their* ministry. She is at that point serveable, and he is willing to serve.

There is a level of marital euphoria which comes when two people are welded together in a mutual dream. They are committed to ideals for which they would gladly die. For some it is the building of a discipling relationship with a group of high school young people; for others it is the conducting of a Bible study of neighbors. For a third couple, it is investment in the lives of children. But there is a joint ministry, and the two share it together.

Serveability grows if there is a level of "pleaseability." There is joy in serving one who is thankful for being served. In our book about birds at home there is a reference to a style of "unpleaseability":

> The male housewren is a habitual nest starter. He stuffs any likely nesting cavity with twigs, grass, and other materials perhaps to mark his territory and perhaps as an inducement to the females when they arrive.
>
> As soon as they appear, the busy male sings to draw their attention. He courts one ardently, wings quivering, tail flickering straight up. If she proves receptive, he escorts her around his prospective nest sites.
>
> The female almost always disapproves of her mate's homebuilding efforts. After she selects one of his sites, she usually removes all the materials and starts the

nest all over again. Sometimes she collects strange items. One nest contained 52 hairpins, 188 nails, 4 tacks, 13 staples, 10 pins, 11 safety pins, 6 paperclips, 2 hooks, 3 garterfasteners, and a buckle.[15]

Talk about hard to please. One can see the forlorn shake of the male's head, after all his hard work, as he sees his new wife completely tear apart his creative efforts. I suspect that one could also imagine his irritation every time he steps on one of the tacks.

There have to be those times when we declare our thanksgiving for the servanthood efforts of our marital partner. We have to show how we are growing in the atmosphere of their love, and we have to say thank you.

Recently, I took a couple of days to retreat by myself for the purposes of study and prayer. One of the things I did on my retreat was to compose a letter to my wife. In it I outlined the great themes of our relationship and what Gail had done over the years to build up my personal life. It took several hours to write, but it was worth each minute because I was able to put my finger on the ways God has used her to shape me. "How do you say 'thank you' for many years of service?" I wrote. "The words seem far too small to describe the appreciation in my heart. Perhaps the fact that I have measurably grown in the sunshine of your love is the best way there is to say, 'I appreciate what you've done!'"

It was this kind of spirit that moved Mary Carolyn Davies to write:

> I love you
> Not only for what you are,
> But for what I am
> When I am with you.
>
> I love you
> Not only for what
> You have made of yourself,
> But for what

You are making of me.

I love you
For the part of me
That you bring out;
I love you
For putting your hand
Into my heaped-up heart
And passing over
All the foolish, weak things
That you can't help
Dimly seeing there,
And for drawing out
Into the light
All the beautiful belongings
That no one else had looked
Quite far enough to find.

I love you because you
Are helping me to make
Of the lumber of my life
Not a tavern
But a temple;
Out of the works
Of my every day
Not a reproach
But a song. . . .[16]

Ms. Davies has tapped the genius of servanthood. In those conditions we grow, and we become what God wants us to be.

SEXUALITY:
TO KNOW

THREE OF MY COLLEGE YEARS WERE SPENT working at night for a trucking company. Among the types of cargo that moved through our terminal were explosives shipped by the military and the mining industry. There was a special tension in the air when we knew that explosives were parked nearby. Strict standards were observed regarding smoking, speeds at which dynamite-laden trailers could be pulled, and the training of men who could handle the loads. We knew that explosives could be either our friend or enemy. That choice was ours to make by our handling of the load; the commodity was neutral. If we kept the rules, the explosives were an asset; if we broke them, the asset could suddenly become a disastrous liability.

When I take up the subject of sexuality in marriage, I sense the same choice. Sex is a volatile subject because it is like our explosives. It is man's friend or it becomes his enemy. It is his servant or his master. Similarly, sex is neutral in character; we who use it determine its ultimate status as maker or destroyer.

It is no secret that a tremendous preoccupation exists among people about the subject of sex. I don't think it has ever been any different. I'm sure that many readers who scanned the table of contents of this book turned first to this chapter with its heading about sex. Somehow sex speaks to our curiosity faster than the other topical headings. (I remember seeing a greeting card with a colorful front cover featuring one word: "SEX!!!" When the reader opened it up, he felt foolish as he read, "Now that I've got your attention, I'd like to say a few things.")

No one passes through a day without being confronted with the appeal to our sexual appetites. Advertising, styles of dress, the overall sensual theme of our culture all conspire to set in motion our sexual instincts. The stimuli to our sexual drives abound, and many people find themselves constantly trying to master the struggle they have of mental preoccupation, fantasy, or lust. Unless you journey to the North Pole, you probably won't be able to escape the problem, and even there you'll have your memories to contend with.

I think of this as a day of sexual tyranny when every possible sexual weapon is being employed to gain our attention. My observation is that the conflict is reducing many Christian men and women to a painful sense of guilt and frustration. There are many reasons for this, and one of them centers on the fact that the church has been scandalously remiss in dealing with the subject of sex with proper candor. We have set forth a few rules that are obvious to everyone and hoped that no one would ask any personal questions. If one finds it hard to agree with my point, just let him sit in a Sunday school class the day the lesson comes from the book of Galatians and a young lady raises her hand during the question period to ask the teacher, "What does the word *circumcision* mean?"

For reasons we cannot explore in this book, Christians have not handled the subject of sex gracefully. Our very silence has made the subject seem terribly dirty. We appear to the world to be a tradition which is antisexual. Only the Shakers of old who rejected all forms of physical passion seem to have outpointed us in our emptiness on the subject.

Does it seem that I am hard to please when I say that I see a sudden plethora of books coming out of Christian publishing houses which seem to be trying to make up for lost time? People appear to be coming out of the walls with Christian literary parallels to *The Sensuous Woman* and *Everything You Always Wanted to Know About Sex But Were Afraid to Ask.* Some of them seem to be very pleasant books, packaged to sell well, but I get the feeling that we are skimming the thin surface of a subject. There is very little attempt to get beneath the surface to find out why we are sexual and why we possess such strong sexual appetites. More than one man has admitted that his struggle is not to find out how to perform sexually; it is rather why he feels so constantly compelled to perform. What is this thing which pulls so hard and actually tempts people to jeopardize an entire career, lifelong relationships, and a specially crafted reputation in exchange for a few moments of physical pleasure?

According to Dr. Gary Collins, Paul Tournier has studied the subject of sexual attitudes and discovered four basic categories of thinking.

There are those, first of all, who devaluate sexuality, reducing it to the mere level of glandular function. They see it as an act stimulated and consummated in the same way animals act instinctively. The urge is biological; the experience is biological.

A second group deifies sexuality, overestimating its importance, judging all experience from this perspective. Call these the pleasure-seekers, characterized best of all by the stunning quote of one starlet known for her unbridled sexual life, who said, "I don't feel that I can really judge the character of a man until I've had sex with him."

The third group in Tournier's classification of sexual attitudes considers sex as necessary but contemptible. Apart from the process of procreation, excessive sexual experience may jeopardize one's physical health and mental alertness—so goes their theory.

A final group looks at sex through what I would like to call the eyes of biblical attitude. These would admit that sex is biological in some sense. They could agree that sex is immensely pleasurable. But, bypassing the third attitude altogether, they go on to another point as yet unmade: that the fullness and wholeness of sexual experience is the *result* of a relationship, not the beginning or the entirety of one. This is entirely contrary to a present trend in sexual thinking.

It is Rollo May in his book *Love and Will* who notes that the *performance* of sex has progressively become more important than the meaning or gratification of sexual experience. The premium is now placed on the number of possible orgasms, the acrobatic varieties of sexual position, and the various allowable deviations from the basic sexual act. Drs. Masters and Johnson, the St. Louis sex researchers, have lately spoken out with alarm about this trend. They warn that the culture is headed for sexual disaster because it does not realize that pure, unrestrained physical copulation, apart from some sense of previous quality to the relationship, has destructive results.

The Bible told us this a long time ago. But it was rejected by many who didn't want to hear. And it was often misinterpreted by others who heard only what they wanted to hear. But let the Bible speak for itself, and one gains a beautiful new perspective on the meaning of sexual union.

The Meaning of Sexual Union

Moses tells us in Genesis 2:23 that when Adam saw Eve, he cried out, "*At last,* this is flesh of my flesh, bone of my bone." Adam is excited because now he can relate to someone whose heart pulsates like his. This is a relationship not like the vertical one with God, whom he worships; and it isn't like the one he has with the animals, whom he dominates. But it is a relationship with someone like him—flesh and bone—whom he will neither worship nor dominate. He will serve her, serve with her, and share with her.

Remember Moses' commentary on Adam's joy: this is why, Moses writes, men leave their fathers and mothers. They mature to a point where they sense "aloneness," something which cannot be found in the old parental relationship. It causes them to groan inwardly for a relationship with someone who will be flesh and bone with them. This, Moses says, is why men cleave to a wife: *to search out and recover Adam's relational joy.*

Remember, also, that I suggested that Adam was always one-flesh with Eve. But his one-flesh was more than physical copulation. It was one-flesh on the emotional, the intellectual, and the spiritual level. Much of this was seriously impaired when sin entered their lives.

Before sin Adam had a natural hunger to cleave to Eve. I suspect that the force of our sexual drive may be a sample of the kind of force or hunger Adam had for his wife on all of the levels we have been discussing. He craved romance, companionship, and servanthood every bit as much as he craved sexual relationship. It may also be a sample of how men hungered for God. But when sin devastated all of the relationships between God and man, and man and other men, all of man's hunger to cross to others on each level was virtually destroyed, leaving only the physical experience behind. Bereft of his intellectual and spiritual capacities, man resorted to his one strong capacity, the physical. Thus our sex drive often exists in strength out of balance with the other seriously weakened hungers and capacities within us to relate to others. Many times, therefore, the only thing that provides restraint on man's physical appetites is the social controls that we have put upon ourselves in our communities.

But the more man senses the intellectual barrenness of the modern era, and the more he suffers from the effects of spiritual sterility, the more he is led to return to the physical for some kind of an *"at last"* experience. This is the end of every culture, and Paul is not unmindful of that as he traces the demise of sinful men in Romans, chapter one. In the final analysis, it comes down to physical gratification when the God of creation is abandoned or ignored. And when one gets to the physical level, Paul says, he not only becomes absorbed in sexual experience, but he may need to pervert it, draining from it every conceivable variety. It is the only thing he has left; he has to make use of it if he is to find anything like the "at last" which Adam found in Eve. But in the long run it's too little, and it's far too late.

The more one pursues the "at last" on a purely physical basis, the more lonely he becomes. Our whole culture has become what sociologist David Riesman once called a lonely crowd. We are lonelier than ever in our massive homes and wild schedules. Our early American need to lean on each other for sheer survival—as on the frontier and in agricultural communities—has ceased to be necessary. At least our mutual concern for survival then brought the wagons together if an attack was on, brought people together for a barn raising or a harvest. That was a kind of glue of relationship. But even that doesn't exist any longer.

There is simply no longer a need-meeting form of communication. The more a person realizes this the more he must reach out of his loneliness and reach somebody somehow. One of the ways one hopefully reaches out is through sex. Seeking the "at last," the only facility left reasonably intact—the physical—goes into action. A person's desire to relate sexually increases greatly. His attraction to pornographic literature and photography, for example, are ways in which he tries to communicate—even if it is with someone on paper whom he'll never meet, never touch, and with whom he'll never share. Perhaps in looking at a naked body, he may find a momentary escape from loneliness. But it is a kind of "at last" which doesn't last. And because it is so one-dimensional and so short-lived, he can only seek more and more of the same, always hoping that the next film, the next page, the next story will bring that relationship which something deep in his heart tells him is out there. What he seeks is the "at last" God created us to experience but which will never be found apart from God's place in our lives.

In a fascinating little book called *Alone at High Noon* Professor Emile Cailliet recalls the tragic life of Charles Baudelaire, the French poet. Baudelaire apparently perverted his sexual life in every conceivable way until, Cailliet says, "he suffered from moral misery." Surveying his own emptiness, Baudelaire wrote, "After a debauch, one always feels more lonely, more deserted."

That is exactly my point when I say that the misuse of the sexual capacity always ends in a revived and continuous hunger and thirst for more frequent and diverse physical relationships which simply will not be quenched. Driven deeper and deeper into an inner emptiness, Baudelaire illustrates the extreme spiritual poverty in which many people are living today. His own agony is revealed when he writes, and Cailliet quotes,

Do you hear these sighs, preludes to a tragedy of dishonor, these wails, these cries, these rattlings in the throat? Who has not proffered them, who has not irresistibly extorted them? Is there anything worse in the cross-examinations of torturers? These reversed sleepwalker's eyes, these limbs, whose muscles tremble and stiffen as beneath the action of a galvanic battery. Drunkenness, delirium and opium in their most violent reactions certainly do not furnish such frightful and curious examples. And the human face, which Ovid believed to be made to reflect the stars, there it is with no more than an expression of mad ferocity, or distended in a sort of death. *Surely I should commit a sacrilege to apply the word "ecstasy" to this kind of "decomposition."* [17]

The Old Testament was not unaware of man's problem. It clearly shows us the pursuit of the "at last" by a number of people. We find it employing two different verbs to describe the sexual experience of men and women who communicate purely on a physical level and those who in the plan of God seek communion on all levels and experience sexual relationship as the result.

When men and women are described in the Bible as having sexual experience, the verb most often used is translated, in many versions, "to know." Our English

MAGNIFICENT MARRIAGE

translation "intercourse" has simply lost all meaning for
us to see the message in that Old Testament verb. "To
know" is exactly what God meant for the sexual act to
be: human beings relating to each other not only on the
physical level but mentally, emotionally, and spiritually.
The "to know" experience is an exercise of the total
human communication. It is the "at last" of which Adam
spoke. Thus, Adam *knew* Eve; Abraham *knew* Sarah,
and on both occasions there were children. In each case
the Old Testament is telling us: these people enjoyed
the ultimate experiences of human communion.

The second Old Testament verb which describes sex
is translated "to lie with." Joseph was propositioned by
Potiphar's wife with the words "Come lie with me."
When David committed adultery, it is said, "He lay with
Bathsheba." This is in considerable contrast to the first
verb. It is an externalized description of two bodies
copulating together, more a biological or physical act
than anything else. It is as if the verb is saying, if you
could see them, you'd know everything there is to know.
There is no internalizing of relationship in this experience. It is devoid of communication on all the levels
we've described. It is a devalued experience which may
satisfy the physical (and maybe briefly the emotional),
but will never let a man cry out with the long-range
conviction, "at last." The inner void of aloneness will
soon return, and the "lie-with" experience must be
repeated again and again to put a stop to the need.

The "lie-with" act is a counterfeit action. It is akin to
the little child who plays house, trying to create all the
feelings of what it is like to be a mother and homemaker.
The action is real; the experience is shallow. On the
other hand, the "to know" is genuine, and it is far
broader and expansive than just the physical act. Perhaps it could be compared to the experience of climbing
a mountain. There is a climber's ecstasy at the summit,
as there is an ecstasy in the moments of sexual relations.

But in both cases the summit experience is what it is because of the climb behind it. The struggle, the planning, the pain, and the exhaustion were all part of the climb, and the thrill at the summit is compounded by the price that was paid to get there.

Imagine with me two climbers who have groped their way to a precarious summit on a climb that lasted three days. They have braved danger, fought the cold, and said "no" to a thousand temptations to turn back. As they stand there triumphantly taking in the view their struggle has procured for them, a helicopter appears. It approaches the summit and discharges two passengers. They also stand on the summit and experience the same view. In that same moment both pairs of human beings stand on the same ground, feel the same wind, see the same topography. They gasp at the beautiful panorama. But you may already sense with me that there is a difference between the two experiences. One ecstasy is marked by the previous three-day climb and its accomplishments. The other ecstasy is relatively cheap. No pain, just an airborne bounce which cost nothing but money and a few minutes of time. You simply cannot equate the two experiences just because their momentary act of standing on the summit appears to be similar. The route and the price of getting there make all the difference in the world.

In searching out the biblical approaches to sex, we've mentioned two verbs: "to know" and "to lie with." There is a third: "to go in to." When Abraham made the serious mistake of impregnating Hagar, his wife's servant, to produce a son, he was doing something that was common in that culture. If a wife appeared to be barren, a husband was permitted to try to have a son by a woman selected by his wife. The act of bringing her to pregnancy is described here as *to go in to.* This verb seems to imply sexual intercourse for one purpose only, to plant semen in the womb for the sake of having children. I think it is important to highlight this fact, for by comparing these verbs, we can see that God had a bigger view of sex than just making babies or having a few moments of pleasure. The sex God portrays in Scripture did, on occasion, make babies; it certainly was pleasurable; but it crossed the whole spectrum of human communion, and when it was the result of a relationship of cleaving, it was properly named. It was the experience of *knowing*, and that is what God wants us to experience because it is not good for us to live alone.

The Message of Sexuality

I would like to propose the idea that there are three messages which are transmitted when husband and wife "know" one another. There is a message of love given from husband to wife. There is a second message in the opposite direction: wife to husband. But there is a third message: it is the message of the relationship mutually to both people. For "knowing" is a special event in the lives of married people. And set in the biblical conditions, it transmits to the innermost being of each person in the experience something of ultimate and eternal significance.

To begin with, "knowing" depends on an unbreakable connection between the physical and the spiritual elements of the person. That connection centers on the concept of *commitment*. Commitment is that act of "forsaking all others and keeping yourself only for him or her." It begins as an act of renunciation from all other potentially interfering relationships, and it depends upon the ongoing act of renunciation of those relationships.

There is something within us, hard to locate or define, which craves commitment. Rarely are human beings more emotionally struck than when they are called to attention about some commitment. Perhaps we have a tear or two when the flag is raised, or we read the description of a moving death scene in which two lovers are being separated. We are excited by a team which plays hard together, and we admire the person—perhaps an artist or an author—who has made a commitment to master a discipline and execute it with excellence. Something there is about us that is attracted to the concept of commitment.

Conversely, when commitments are broken, we are startled. A football player leaves a team for another to earn more money, and it jolts us—not in the mind, for in the rational sense it is a simple conclusion: more money. It is our attraction to commitment which bothers us. We hurt to see an Ann Landers announce her divorce; somehow we thought she'd mastered commitment if anybody had.

Why are we moved by commitment; and why are we bothered over noncommitment? I like to think the answer pivots on the fact that God made us to be committed people. A keystone of our very essence as human beings is the hunger to commit ourselves and to have others commit themselves to us. I am being neither theological or psychological when I say—for the purpose of setting out the concept—that there is within us a "commitment apparatus." Perhaps it could be called an inmost "holy of holies," into which we admit an extraordinarily limited number of people.

It is with this commitment apparatus, this area I call the holy of holies, that we dwell in peace with God and where we invite those of intimate association. Real "knowing" happens when we choose to give a key to this area to God and to a special person. I suspect that we give this key over to only one God and to one person if we wish to keep that area only for the purposes of "knowing."

In the performance of the sexual act, we physically symbolize the entire dynamic of giving the key over and entering into the holy of holies with another person. We enter one another, and we "know."

When we "lie with," we symbolize the giving over of the key, but we do not open the door. We are saying, "touch me externally, but do not come to the door of my internal holy of holies." To shift analogies, we keep trying to reach the top of the mountain without facing the struggles of the climb. What happens is a momentary *feeling* of "knowing" but a long-term dissatisfaction.

We are made to make very few commitments of the "knowing" variety—in fact, normally only one. The Bible says that this commitment is made to one person and is broken only by death. If it is broken by divorce or infidelity, the succeeding experiences of "knowing" will be less than totally satisfactory.

The promiscuous person rejects this law of commitment, and gives the key to the holy of holies to many people. It is as if he distributed master keys to a personal area actually only big enough for one to enter. In our general relationships with friends, we allow some to come near to our holy of holies, but only one can enter the most intimate part. I might add that even that one person cannot come all the way because we are sinners and incapable of perfect commitment. That possibility was devastated by the sin of Adam.

Distribute too many keys to your holy of holies, and it becomes less sacred. The experience of "knowing" loses its intensity. Now the commitment apparatus in the holy of holies of our lives is dirtied, misused, and once soiled, it can rarely recover completely.

A young woman married nine years illustrated this observation when she related to me her inability to desire or experience sexual fulfillment with her husband. Her distress was growing because she saw her husband's frustration. He blamed himself for her inability to be sexually satisfied; he thought he was less than "what a man should be." Her distaste for sex, she admitted, began less than six months after their wedding. After I had ascertained that her husband was not forcing upon her sexual experiences which were crude or painful, I ventured to ask about her premarital experiences with sex. It was difficult for her, but she finally shared the facts of several sexual experiences with two or three young men in the process of dating. Some months before her marriage to her husband, she and her fiancé had engaged in sexual activity with growing frequency as the wedding date approached. Marriage, they reasoned, was just around the corner.

What began to unravel in our conversation was her inability to cope with her shame at having allowed her body to be surrendered in moments of sexual appetite and passion. Her desire to be accepted by a man, to enjoy some sort of instant security, had overcome the defenses of the holy of holies which did not wish to admit anyone unless a commitment had been made. But as the holy of holies was violated by several different men, her commitment apparatus began to react violently. It began to send to her conscious mind more and more messages of protest; it threw up stronger and stronger defenses against letting anyone in. When a commitment was indeed made in marriage, the patterns of resistance at the door were already too strong to overcome, and now entering into the holy of holies was not a pleasant experience.

You can begin now to picture with me what has happened. A woman's ability "to know" has been severely hampered. The commitment apparatus has been misused; the door to the holy of holies has been barred. A physical drive within says to go through the door; a spiritual drive, the commitment apparatus says, "no way!" She has lost the ability "to know" and will have to be content "to lie with," until something of a remedy can be found.

When the door of the holy of holies has been reinforced by our commitment apparatus, a person is left with three possible alternatives. The first two are bad.

The first thing one can do is cut the line between the physical and the spiritual altogether—as I've already observed—and "lie with." This is like marching to the door of the holy of holies and simply kicking down the door once and for all. Kick down enough of the door, and anyone can enter. And this is quite possible to do. We've just described what a promiscuous person does. Kick down the door, distribute master keys; it's all the same.

Theologically, this is the dulling of the conscience. Reject the message of the conscience long enough, and it will cease to speak. From that time forth, one can freely use his or her body in sexual experience, gaining pleasure at the summit for a few moments each time. But they will never "know." They will only "lie with," and the satisfaction will be quite shallow.

The second possibility when facing the barred holy of holies is to let it stay shut. Cut the power lines to the spiritual and physical drives which crave "knowing," and do nothing. Just play the game of resistance. Be tired, find excuses, get sick, break out in a cold sweat, project blame upon the other person. It is all part of the symptoms of a person who has closed and nailed over the doors and windows of the holy of holies and never faces the challenge of "knowing" again.

The Bible has not pulled its punches in regards to these kinds of people. We have the frank description of David's son, Amnon, in 2 Samuel 13. This young man had virtually everything he wished. But suddenly he found something he couldn't have: his half sister, Tamar. Such was his lust for her that he literally expended vast amounts of energy in pure inner desire. His style of life had been so indulged that it could not bear being refused; it was as if all kinds of circuits and relays blew when he was turned down.

To finally get Tamar, he mounted an elaborate plot to get her to his apartment, where he raped her. The fall-out of the moment was dramatic. His desire was only "to lie with," for the moment he withdrew from her, the Bible says, he was filled with contempt for her. He had violated her holy of holies by kicking down the door, and when he was through, he was emptier than ever. The summit had been reached in a quick, violent jump, and it was ugly.

When we last hear from Tamar she is a disillusioned woman. She seems to have been willing to go through the process of commitment with Amnon, but he didn't want sex on that basis. Now she sees herself soiled and cheapened. Never again would "knowing" be a possibility without going back to that time when her right to open the door was stolen by someone who wished to kick it down.

The young woman with whom I was counseling had a third alternative, and it was the one we pursued. She could face the fact that her earlier sexual activities outside of commitment were, by God's definition of relationship, sin. This could be confessed and forgiven. When we knelt and prayed, I was able to affirm that, according to God's promises, she had been forgiven. I wanted her now to go home and begin actions of affection toward her husband which might begin to regenerate the commitment processes. I warned her that it would be some time before she would be able to overcome the feeling of sexual repugnance completely, but if she reaffirmed her forgiveness on each occasion that the adverse impulses arose, perhaps she could break through the barriers herself and thus allow her husband to join her in her holy of holies. Slowly she was able to do this, and many months later she and her husband were able to report that their sexual experiences were becoming what they had always sought them to be. They were no longer "lying with"; they were "knowing."

When the climbers struggle to the summit, it is a moment of ecstasy. They have enjoyed the challenge of the climb, and they celebrate the success of the ascent at the top. When they begin the descent, each step seems a bit lighter and more enjoyable because they have been to the summit. The summit experience looks both backward to establish its worth, and it looks forward in that it projects joy·in the future of the descent. Sexual experience in "knowing" does the same thing. Its depth of satisfaction rests in the climb; but as it ends, it makes the descent back into the valley of routine living all the easier and more enjoyable. On the descent there will be talk about the time in the near future when once again there can be a meeting on the summit.

The message of biblical sexuality is then one of commitment. It demands a beginning of commitment and a continuity of commitment. Without that unreserved fidelity to one another, "knowing" will be reduced to "lying with." With it, the genius of commitment is affirmed, and our very being fulfills that for which God has made us.

The Role of Sexuality

More than one person who has been hurt in the sexual experience has cried out in frustration, "Why did God give us sex anyway? It does nothing but cause me grief."

If you are not bored with my picture of the climbers, will you come one final time to the summit and listen with me to their triumphant conversation. They point out to each other the route which they have taken. They gasp at the steep inclines they roped themselves up. They remember a tiny meadow where they camped. They treat themselves to a sight that only the climber can fully appreciate. They are celebrating their mutual accomplishment. That's it! A moment of celebration.

Why did God give us sex? It is the supreme moment

of human celebration. The sexual experience is the explosive moment when a husband and wife, committed to each other, symbolize all that they have achieved in their walk together. That is why I have emphasized that sexual "knowing" must be the *result* of a relationship, not the *cause.* If we are trying to cause a relationship through sex—i.e., a young girl trying to get a boyfriend—the emphasis has to be on *performance,* our ability *to do* the sexual act well. But if the sexual experience is the result of the relationship, the emphasis is upon the *gratification* it brings.

Having been committed to one another, we have earned the right to ascend to the summit. In the great and small acts of the day we have affirmed our fidelity to each other. Now we celebrate, and our bodies witness with our spirits, our spirits with our bodies. Perhaps what we are talking about on the highest plane of thinking is this: that sexual "knowing" is the worship service of marriage. We have "assembled together" to rehearse the great acts of our walk with one another, and in one grand embrace we pictorialize the heaped-up pile of commitments and affirmations—the pursuit of one flesh—by becoming physically one flesh.

The worship service in a church is a moment when the bride of Christ—actually, the family of God—becomes one flesh with the Lord in worship. Perhaps God gave us the sexual experience not only to make it possible for us to affirm our own communion in marriage, but to understand the nature of the relationship we have with him. As we have intimacy with one another, we have such intimacy with God. The road to both intimacies is very much alike, and one tells us about the other.

It is conceivable that some could be shocked by this line of thinking, but is it possible that the sexual relationship may be after all the supreme marital sacrament? As a church worship service celebrates the works of God in our lives during the previous week and looks with hope to the coming week of anticipated service, can the sexual embrace provide the same basic experience in marriage? The explosive moment of physical affection may be, if it is in the "knowing" category, the purest moment in the marital life, for "knowing" highlights all of the past and future of what God created us to be and to do. If the worship service highlights the past and coming week, the sexual experience reflects the events of the past day or two and prepares a couple for the next few tomorrows.

Move just a step further in your thinking with me. Perhaps I have come to the point where I can learn something wonderful about my fellowship with God through the sexual experience of "knowing" with my spouse. Worship of the living God has taught me something about ultimate fellowship with my partner in marriage, and my experience in marriage has taught me something about what worship of God is all about. How beautiful is God's way of pulling all things together, teaching us through parallel experience what each dimension of fellowship means.

What makes a part of this difficult to fully settle in our minds is the whole problem of sexual desire, however. Christian people are told that sex is a very sacred thing. But simply telling them that does not help during those moments when a person is paralyzed with sexual stimulation. His guilt level soars as he finds himself preoccupied with overwhelming thoughts about sexual liaison with some attractive person on the street, in the office, or even in a magazine.

Those with a low view of sexual significance have no trouble with this at all. Man is made up of biological drives, they say, and this is all part of the instinct to preserve the species. But for those who follow the God of the Bible, the problem of sexual desire has a far different explanation.

Remember that I previously suggested that the sexual drive may be the leftover dimension of the far more expansive hunger Adam had to "know" Eve before the fall into sin. The reverberation of that rebellion dulled the intellectual and spiritual capacities of man to communicate. Only the physical level remained relatively untouched and capable of functioning as it once did. The physical now out-pushes and out-shoves the other levels for attention. So powerful has it become because it is left unchecked, that it is possible for a person—when unhindered by moral and spiritual values—to reach out and copulate with virtually anyone.

What checks our physical hunger for sexual experience is an all-out effort of the mind when it demands attention for some project the person is interested in (such as a special work deadline, or a creative urge) or the strong legal or traditional protests made by a society in its norms of behavior at one time or another. The Chinese, in their first two decades of rebuilding what they call a New China, seem to have been able to effect a temporary sublimation of the sex drive with a massive commitment to a revolutionary spirit. The other check to our physical hunger comes when we take into our spiritual dimension a commitment to God's laws, and the Holy Spirit makes it plain to us what are the implications of that obedience.

Frequently I hear someone suggest that men are not necessarily monogamous. The evolutionary view is that we have come from an earlier history where men experienced a variety of unrestricted sexual encounters. The theory says that we as a society evolved to a one-man/one-woman ethic simply to keep the peace. Women, on the other hand, it is offered, are probably less prone to the wandering eye because they sense in that lifestyle a lack of security and stability which it is necessary for them to have as childbearers.

But the Bible teaches the exact opposite. Man was created to be monogamous, and the human desire should be for one basic marriage relationship. But rebellion sent that creative design into a tailspin. Man has not evolved; he devolved, going from monogamy to a kind of promiscuous polygamy as a result of sin. Unable to "know" one person, he substitutes the "lie with" as a stopgap measure to touch the relational hunger pangs of the heart. Traditionally, women have not fallen so deep into the trap of illicit sexual desire as men, and this is probably due to their awareness of the enormous consequences of pregnancy and the ensuing need for stability should a child be born. It is interesting to observe that, with the growing decline of respect for motherhood, there is an increase in the acceptance of female promiscuity.

It is sobering to think that God has created me to crave a one-flesh relationship with my wife. The same desire for someone else, the Bible calls lust. Lust is the one-dimensional—thus unchecked—search for fellowship. It is a quest for a counterfeit fellowship. It steps outside the bounds of God's laws and paves a freeway to ultimate moral and spiritual destruction. You can begin to see why a society left with nothing but physical relationships from which to gain satisfaction will simply satiate itself with more and more sexual stimulation.

Perhaps then we can begin to perceive why it is to the distinct advantage of the enemies of God to flaunt before the human race every possible lure to lust, promiscuity, and perversion. Each day the holy of holies of our lives are assaulted with more sexual stimulation. We are told bigger and bigger lies as we are bombarded with freely narrated stories of people who are doing all sorts of "exciting things" and claim they are getting away with it. We are challenged to take every opportunity to join them in it. And the more we give in, the faster our commitment apparatus is defused and rendered inoperative. We become hardened, unable to face self or others, and finally we break into a swift run from the presence of God.

When all of this happens, we not only forfeit our "knowing" capability with a spouse, but we let go of our chance to make great statements of witness to the world about the love of Christ. Once dulled on the horizontal, our commitment capacities are effectively destroyed on the vertical—our relationship to Heaven. The one therefore who perverts and reroutes our sexual make-up, effectively reduces our walk with God, bringing it to a standstill.

It is a widening and wicked circle. As men and women grow more resistant to commitment, the fruits of resistance pervade the culture. Result: more promiscuity. No wonder Paul describes the classic fall of a society in sexual terms. He points out the downward spiral in the book of Romans, chapter one. Man rejects God, the Creator, and he begins to become preoccupied with aspects of the creation itself. He chooses a view of a closed universe, one in which *he* is lord and God is dethroned. All of this downward look of the eyes becomes reflected in man's growing dissatisfaction for normal sexual relationships. Before long his sexual mores take on a greater and greater desire for homosexual experiences and all other sorts of perversions.

Don't be surprised, therefore, as you watch the media saturating our entertainment with tales in dramatic and comedy form of various types of sexual distortion and slanting the story in such a way that you find yourself defending the right of some person to be a homosexual or a transsexual. Don't be surprised when you notice how clever the script-writer is in making the Christian view of sex to look like such a rigid, unhealthy, and even hysterically funny—if not "ancient"—view of things. Cripple our capacity to commit ourselves, and you have paralyzed our ability to know God *and* each other.

But in the aftermath of a *"knowing"* experience, there is something different. Bodies and minds are refreshed in a special and beautiful fatigue. It is as if cool winds have been allowed to blow through the relationship and delight both. The love and commitment is washed clean and reaffirmed. Husband and wife are satisfied. The pornographer may be able to duplicate for us on the screen or the page of the book some methods of performance. He may be able to recreate the sights and sounds of sex, but he can never create the aftermath of freedom and fulfillment which "knowing" brings at the marital summit. It cannot happen in a brothel; it happens in a home.

The Ground Rules
of Knowing

We wish to be free to "know" another person in marriage. Isn't it interesting that many people have entered into marriage and still haven't found the freedom to "know." Walking the aisle and saying some words is not a guarantee that we'll "know." Why? Why are many marriage partners still searching for the freedom to know one another?

Perhaps the answer can be found in our understanding of freedom. We thought freedom was to do what you wish. But then we begin to learn, perhaps through bad experiences, that freedom is best understood when we know the limits. The freedom to know is based on following the ground rules which God has set in motion for "knowing." Follow the ground rules and you experience freedom to know; violate the ground rules, and the counterfeit experience which follows leads one into a kind of captivity. Let me suggest a list of biblical ground rules.

Don't be alarmed if I suggest, at the risk of repetition, that the first rule is *unreserved commitment.* This ground rule comes right from the Ten Commandments: "Thou shalt not commit adultery." This is God's thrust into a sinful world to corral unrestrained passions and instincts and describe the nature of marriage and family for us. In a day when most people felt free to take anyone they wished sexually, God said, you're violating one of the ground rules by which I created relational man.

Pagan man had little concept of this one-man/one-woman idea. This commandment reestablishes the Garden order, a nuclear family in which a fence is built around the relationship. Once the fence is entered, no one goes outside of it again until death.

There are many things men and women can do physically outside of marriage. We shake each other's hands, perhaps embrace in friendship and joy. Some feel free in various cultures to share a kiss. These expressions change everywhere with the culture. I may quickly hug the wife of a close friend here in the United States, but I would not do such a thing in another country where touching another man's wife is seriously frowned upon.

But while there are physical expressions which are permissible in the culture, the Bible draws the line at sexual union. Here we forsake all others; we shut them out from our holy of holies. No exception! Part of the dynamic of sexual experience is that we trust each other about this commitment. We are never the same if we realize that our partner has allowed someone else to enter into that part of his being. The sanctity is not the same anymore.

But this commitment is not only for the sake of shutting others out, but it also involves inviting one another in the relationship in. Paul writes:

> The husband is not lord of his body, but his wife is lord; and the wife is not lord of her body, but her husband is lord. 1 Corinthians 7:3-5.

In these words Paul tells us that one of the acts of marriage is the giving of our bodies to each other sexually as a way of saying, I have given you my entire life. Short of laying down our lives in death for each other, we do this. In the sexual act I am symbolizing my unreserved commitment: I am handing over the title deed of my body, my holy of holies. I say to my spouse, because I know that you love me, I trust you to use my body as you think best for both of us. I become hurtable, exploitable, but I know that you will neither hurt nor exploit me. I trust you to do only the best things for us. In this way I say to you that I am yours.

Many couples have experienced the terrible frustration at this point in their sexual relationships. They have not matured to the point where they can surrender their bodies as Paul describes. Because of unsound teaching or because of distorted sexual thinking, they withhold the full giving of their bodies.

This is a struggle for women, for example, who feel embarrassed about their bodies out of an overemphasized concept of modesty, or an overplayed idea of the nature of physical beauty. They may also have misunderstood the pleasurable aspects of sex. They resist the idea of their husbands fondling each part of their body or even of him visually appreciating the sight of them. Their participation in the sexual act is without freedom, and they find themselves going only as far as is necessary to gratify their husbands, but not so far that they can say they actually enjoy it.

While women have tended to suffer from excess modesty in this matter of commitment and freedom, men have tended to be insensitive to their need to reaffirm their commitment to their wives. The husband who subtly compares his wife with the beauty of other women, who never quite allows his wife to know that above all other women he treasures her most of all, is damaging prospects for freedom in their sexual relationship. A wife feels more free with her husband if she trusts him unreservedly. She is sensitive to the slightest vibration of his dissatisfaction with her. There is no freedom when she is not sure that he is absolutely hers.

How beautiful the sexual experience where two have "known" so deep and so well that their love-play is unrestrained. One occasion may last for brief moments; another for a long period of time. When there is "knowing," there is freedom to love differently, to experiment, to soar with the enjoyment of being close to one another's bodies.

When sexual counseling has been sought out, I have always advised couples to give careful attention to the preparation for moments of possible love-play. If it is an evening set aside for sexual "knowing" I advise both partners to bathe, decorate themselves with pleasant smells and attractive garments as they might so desire. My father smiled one day at the remembrance of his grandfather who used to shave each night just before he went to bed. "As a boy," my father said, "I always used to wonder why Grandad used to shave before he went to bed. It seemed like such a useless exercise. Now I know." A husband and wife should be unusually attentive to matters of quietness, privacy, and atmosphere. Physical "knowing" should never be rushed, interrupted, or distracted.

Let me move to a second ground rule. I call it the principle of *acts of previous love.* Modern sex manuals have insisted on the importance of sexual foreplay. What has not been amplified with force, however, is that there is a kind of foreplay that begins, perhaps, twenty-four hours in advance of the summit.

My wife has often said that the preparation for "knowing" begins for a woman at the beginning of the day. She speaks of a husband's treatment of his wife with tenderness and respect during each moment they are together. If he is sensitive, open to her experiences and reflections, if he has praised her in appreciation for what she has done, she is ready to climb to the summit.

This has been a blind spot to many men for whom sex seems to be only a physical experience. If a day has been punctuated with conflict, disrespect, and insensitivity, it will be difficult for a woman to desire sexual experience with her husband. Her approach to sex is quite different from his. She senses, far better than he, the deeper relational aspects of sex if she has maintained a concept of commitment at the door of her holy of holies. Because her approach to sex is both body and soul, she has difficulty desiring sexual experience if her soul has been wounded or left unfed by him during the day. She may be willing to "lie with" him for the sheer need to relieve sexual tensions that he may have, but she will not have a deep desire to "know" him. The previous acts have denied the symbolism of *the* act. His climb to the peak is not a climb; it is a leap, and she may not be prepared to join him at the summit in this fashion.

A wise and loving husband and wife arise in the morning and share the responsibilities of the family as they commence the day. Perhaps praying together, encouraging each other concerning the events to come, they bid each other good-bye. They begin to look forward to their rendezvous that evening when they will shut the door to the world and, finally, to the children and join together in sexual embrace. On occasion it may be mentioned in the morning that this is in the offing for the evening. It becomes something to look forward to, and it becomes throughout the day a cause and effect of intimate relationships with each other.

There are those who are always emphasizing the spontaneity of sex. I emphatically agree that there should be times when sexual relationships result from the sheer enthusiasm of a moment. But never omit the planned times to which you can look forward with some expectancy. They can have a great part in marriage together also.

A third ground rule for "knowing" is *the necessity of clear accounts.* "Knowing" happens in a relationship where there are no unresolved violations. We see this principle spiritually highlighted in Paul's treatment of the problem the Corinthians were having at the communion table. Apparently, the Christians at Corinth felt that the communion was a ritual. They felt perfectly free to eat of the bread and drink the wine when all the time they tolerated terrible divisions, patterns of sin, and spiritual heresies among the congregation. Paul says, "no way!" Bluntly, he points out that a man has to examine himself and his relationships before becoming one flesh with God. He has to confess his sin, and he is in spiritual trouble if he doesn't. Unconfessed sin makes the communion table an empty ritual, a barren religious exercise.

"Knowing" requires the same thing in marriage. There will be no impetus to sexual communion if there are unresolved tensions and actions between husband and wife. If they are large matters, the desire of a wife and husband to embrace will probably be quenched. But what can become dangerous is the failure to resolve small things each day, the things which hurt in the quietness of one's soul. They are often overlooked and therefore untended to. Nevertheless, they build up in the soul. The little irritants in the relationship go on and on, piling up. In the light of unresolved patterns, there may continue to be sexual experience, but little by little the sexual experience results from pure physical desire rather than the summitry of "knowing." What happens is that something which was once "knowing" now becomes "lying with."

I cannot leave this ground rule without pointing out the irony of confession and forgiveness. With the clearing of the relationship of hurts and aches, there is often a stimulus to the act of "knowing." That is why in our discussion on conflict I quoted the phrase "making up is such great fun." It is! With the relief of resolution, there is a beautiful rush to climb to the summit. The relationship is clean again.

Let us go on to the fourth ground rule in "knowing," the *principle of privacy.* Sexual experience cannot be shared with anyone but the partners involved. It is an act designed for two and two alone. One's mind may quickly recall reading in some place about the upsurge in so-called "group sex," play by three or more people at once. Here again is a perfect illustration of the sinful culture's desire to devastate the meaning of relationships and commitment. Seeking only the thrills of the summit, such people reason that if there is fun for two, the fun must be compounded if more enter in. What fools!

"Knowing" can only occur in secret between two. Its pleasurability and satisfaction can be so sublime that one or both might find the impulse to want to talk about it with others, to share the good news of this wonderful thing discovered. But that is exactly what cannot be done. For to share the secret is to dissolve its dynamic. When we have been given the key to each other's hearts, the holy of holies, we do not spread the information of what we found there.

Who is there who hasn't heard the belittling sex-oriented conversations which take place at the beauty shop or the YMCA locker room? You can be sure that the woman complaining about her husband's insatiable sexual appetite or the husband publicly complaining about his wife's sexual reluctance has never "known." They have only "lain with." For when one is truly "known," he guards the key of the experience with his very life.

A fifth ground rule in "knowing" is a derivative of the first one. It is the commitment *to fully please the other person.* You know that you have crossed the line into this ground rule when you are more concerned about pleasing your spouse than you are in pleasing yourself. Do you sense the absolute beauty emerging in this principle? Do you see the crescendo that is reached when two give to each other with complete abandon? We are saying in our action, I am surrendering myself to the ministry to your body and soul, believing that if you are satisfied, I too will be satisfied. When both do this, a full circle emerges. The more I give, the more I receive. This is nothing new. Jesus was making this principle plain two thousand years ago both in his words and deeds. "The last shall be first, the first last," and "He who loses his life shall save it; he who saves it loses it."

The "knowing" sexual experience illustrates that fact in living color.

How radically different from the new morality (perhaps it is very old) which says "get!" rather than give. Hear the disappointment of the woman who sees in sex only the quick act of her husband's gratification. He uses her to exhaust *his* needs and tensions. He never takes the time to discover *her* feelings. As the months and years pass, she resists ever allowing herself to desire sex personally. She will enter into the act for his sake, but never for the joy of her own ability to "know." He wonders why she is sexually turned off, but he never fully contemplates why it is that he is the culprit, not she.

If we have brought into the relationship only what we *think* or might have *heard* from some other source about the needs of our spouse, we will probably never "know." We must communicate and talk with each other about what pleases. We must affirm each other in that act about these things which we enjoy and which bring depth to the experience. But if there is silence, we will never be able to fully please.

I cannot leave this principle of fully pleasing the other without venturing to suggest that it has a correlate. That is that to "know" one another we must be "pleasable." A husband needs to know if he is pleasing his wife. Even a Christian man cannot help but be affected by the world's emphasis upon performance. As a man, one of his personal dimensions of fulfillment is the satisfaction that he can sexually please his wife. How important it is for her to affirm him on these matters, for if she does not, it will be a blight upon his self-image, and it will cause him to try with even greater determination until he finally reaches the pinnacle he seeks: that as a man, his wife finds pleasure in him.

Among the principles that could be studied is a final one which I call *the principle of balance.* This arises out of the well-known fact of the differences between male and female.

In the average marriage relationship, the husband

will normally be the pursuer in matters sexual. He will desire them with much greater significance, and his desire will be fairly consistent.

The wife, on the other hand, will normally be content with a fewer number of sexual experiences, and her level of desire will often be geared to the special points in time in her monthly cycle. This will tend to be more significant than the events of a particular day. A husband, with his constant sexual intensity, may find this fact to be frustrating. And the wife, on the other hand, may find her husband's constant amorous pursuit to be confusing. She may even be tempted to think her husband is abnormal, that he thinks of her only as a body, and that she is only valuable as a sex partner. "Can't I ever satisfy him?" she asks. "Doesn't she really enjoy it as much as I do?" he wonders.

Because of these differences a wife seems, in the perspective of her husband, to be rather coolly detached from sex. He is often bothered and confused about the fact that she does not seem to have the same problems he has with lust. He is disturbed that she seems to be able to have more control over her sexual desire, to be able to say "no!" to whatever sexual drive he imagines her to have. He knows how little power he seems to have over his own sexual push, that he can be aroused by a mere glance, an eyeful of his wife's body, a thought or a memory. Sometimes he makes advances of affection which he is sure will arouse his wife to response, and she merely thanks him for his affection and quietly goes off to sleep. In the meantime he lies awake, wondering about their differences and where he failed. He may even become angry at her, thinking that sexual experience is a detached reality which she can control with an internal switch. Since it is almost impossible for him to do, it makes him momentarily feel distant from her. It may, on occasion, make him feel dirty and ashamed at the vast contrast there seems to be in their abilities to discipline themselves. He may even vow that he is going to give up sex for a few weeks until she admits to having the same desire he does. But normally his vow is forgotten within a day.

The differences also raise speculations within a wife. She does not find it as easy as he does to enter into sexual experience. She wonders if this is all he ever wants from her. Does she lack the capacity to satisfy him enough? Is there always something more to be done, something more to give? Why does everything seem to have a sexual connotation to her husband? Is it just her imagination that he appears to think sexually a large part of the time? She wonders if she is the wrong woman for him. She may even be tempted to dislike sex; it seems to raise so many problems.

Why, she goes on to ask herself, does he not realize that she needs more time to enter into sex? Why does he seem in a rush, and why is it all over so quickly afterwards? Is he abnormal? Is she abnormal?

I am convinced after some years of talking with husbands and wives about these things that it is almost impossible for us to fully understand our differences. We can only pursue balance. Balance begins when we accept one another, not for what we think the other should be, but for what the other is. Within reasonable limits, we should not make value or moral judgments about the other person. Thus a husband learns to sensitize himself to his wife's desires, and perhaps he disciplines his desires just a bit. She, on the other hand, recognizes that there will be times when even though she herself is not aggressively impelled to sexual experience, that it is a time to give. Perhaps she will not achieve total sexual fulfillment, but she can give it to her husband and find a quiet, deeper fulfillment within herself.

It is important to add that a wife with her contrasting appearance of control over her sexual desire should never hold this as a spiritual plus over her husband's head. Some women have done this; they have identified a natural fact about themselves as a mark of maturity, when in fact it wasn't; it was merely the balance of the female.

A husband, on the other hand, should not defend his frequent desires as either a sign of superior sexuality or his wife's frigidity. Either is probably quite wrong and simply demonstrates that he misunderstands her as she does him. In our understanding of the differences, we bring balance into play. And balance arises when we accept each other and become sensitive to what each other really is.

A woman—we'll call her Dolores—visits a counselor and opens up the sordid details behind a sense of intense guilt. She describes her marriage, pointing out that while it was marked with love in most areas of the relationship, the sexual experience was a deep disappointment to her. Since neither husband nor wife had been counseled on sexual matters before their wedding, Dolores recalls that she did not know how to respond when she found their acts of marital love to be painful and unsatisfactory. Unable to confront her husband with the fact that sex was frankly undesirable to her, she pretended on each sexual encounter that she was delighted and fulfilled. Dolores's husband was not perceptive enough to notice the lie.

Dolores's disillusionment and frustration was further heightened each time she read or heard anything about sex which led her to believe that she was missing out on something which seemed relatively obvious and uncomplicated for everyone else in the world.

One night when her husband was gone on a business appointment, she found herself confiding her personal struggles with a woman-friend in the neighborhood, who in turn shared the story with her own husband. It wasn't many days later that the husband contrived a reason to stop by Dolores's house when she was alone and offer his own sexual abilities—as he put it—"to relieve her frustration." At first Dolores was horrified, but the proposition did set in motion thoughts based on curiosity and hurt which uncontrollably swirled in her mind for many days. Within a couple of weeks, Dolores had given in and begun an extramarital affair. Dolores saw her neighbor's husband with weekly frequence, and the meetings carried on for almost a year.

As she talks to the counselor she tearfully evaluates an illicit relationship over which—now that the "glamor" has worn off—she feels destructive guilt. The anticipation of each week's rendezvous, she says, dissolves soon after into depression and regret. Dolores sees no way to end the relationship without several people getting hurt.

If you sit in the counselor's chair for a moment, you will note a series of compounding tragedies in Dolores's marriage. A first note of concern would center on the fact that Dolores and her husband cannot communicate honestly with one another. He apparently has made no attempt to discern his wife's feelings about her sexual life. Preoccupied with himself, he is not sensitive enough to perceive that she is withholding from him some of the most important information there is about her inner being. Why couldn't Dolores talk about her problems with her husband? Is it because he becomes too defensive on such occasions? Because his feelings are hurt too easily? Because he cannot stand to have his masculine image threatened?

What Dolores ended up telling her neighbor, she should have been able to confide to her spouse, but she couldn't, and the sensitive information which she mistakenly released got immediately into the hands of one who could misuse it. What little resistance Dolores had faded quickly because she apparently had scant awareness of how easy it is to exploit lonely persons who have these kinds of problems.

But take a hard look at Dolores after the affair has carried on for a few months and see if the problem has been solved. Those who believe in "to-lie-with" sex never speak about these kinds of results. Dolores had made a "leap" to the summit, feeling that she could not make it up the trail. Her holy of holies had been violated by someone who had no right to enter. As a result her commitment apparatus has rebelled, and the adverse feelings, like earthquake waves, are now fanning out throughout her person. What she had thought to be an antidote to a marital problem was devouring her. Out of the frying pan and into the fire.

Dolores wants out of the relationship. But there is no way out apart from the hurt that will be borne by several other parties. A friendship will be destroyed; a marriage will be in jeopardy. A woman will bear the inner conflicts and memories of an ugly series of acts of betrayal. The momentary excitement of those unlawful times deteriorates now into a morass of bitter regret. Dolores had settled on a "to-lie-with" relationship, thinking it was a freeway to "knowing." But now everything lies shattered.

The Risks and Dangers of Summitry

How beautiful the freedom and ecstasy of lovers! But how dangerous the paths over which they walk. It seems a law of life today that the most beautiful things are the most dangerous. The things which are the most valuable are those which are most frequently counterfeited. The things which cost the most are offered to us at discount prices.

It is *these things* which serve as a final warning about "knowing." A world apart from Jesus Christ seeks everything he offers as long as it can have it *without him*. It wants peace without surrender; it wants freedom without rules. It wants "knowing" without commitment. In a day of improvisation and imitation, it can produce all of these things . . . for a moment. But as in most cheap imitations, the cracks finally show and give way.

The man and woman of today can never "know" apart from Christ. And if the world cannot fully "know" in relationships, it will try to deny that privilege to anyone who would try to ascend the mountain in the right way. For the man or woman who tries the route of commitment, there will often be ridicule and laughter. They will be flooded with statistics, stories, and jokes suggesting that no one is being faithful, why should they? They will be inundated with the "everybody's-doing-it" argument. They will be bombarded by media which report the "happy" lives of people who take new lovers on an annual basis.

We cannot underestimate battle conditions in a world bent on destroying one-flesh relationships. Every time a man leaves his home, he will be confronted with the impressions of advertising, the conversations of people who think they know a better way, and of members of the opposite sex who are not only willing to enjoy the attentions of other men or women, but who by their dress and actions actively seek it.

Godly partners will take this all into account, and rather than *suspect* their spouses, they will *protect* them. It is demeaning to say to a woman that there is competition out there which she must face if she is to keep her husband. Rejecting the statement, she does not realize a more seriously worded warning: there are *traps* out there for her husband. The Bible records the stories of men of God, like David, who fell into those traps and virtually ruined their lives. Thus, a wise woman keeps herself alert not to the competition but to the traps. She makes herself becoming, she keeps her mind sharp, and she keeps her heart open and sensitive to her husband and their God. She does not belittle her husband's weaknesses when she sees them, but rather helps him protect himself against the hidden and subtle pits of this society.

A godly husband gives his wife a firm arm upon which to lean. He keeps himself removed from suspicion; he avoids the places where he could either be tempted or suspected. He respects his wife's mind and judgment. He affirms her for her value as a woman and as a child of God. He is quick to point out the full dimension of her virtues as against the cheap and papier-mâche beauty of the woman who is only a physical specimen of what the world calls beauty. He disciplines his mind and spirit to evaluate beauty, not on the basis of form and structure, but on the basis of character and servanthood.

I see two climbers ascending the mountain, roped together, talking, directing, warning, and encouraging one another. Neither berates the other for small slips or mistakes, but they seek rather to bolster and protect each other. The higher the summit, the harder the climb, the bigger the risks. But when they reach the top, the satisfaction is ecstatic.

I see another couple, not climbing a mountain, but walking from the church where they have just pledged themselves to one another. If what has been said in this book is true, their walk will be a tiptoe affair through a minefield of challenges and opportunities. There will be those who will wish to destroy their walk as if they were cutting the mountain climber's rope. If the couple is to succeed, it will be because they do not walk alone.

An invisible third party will walk with them through the years. It will be Jesus Christ, the Son of God, whom they have invited to be not only Lord of their lives but Lord of their relationship. The things which this book says are necessary for a one-flesh relationship will be absolutely impossible without him. For he is the one who has provided a way for the barriers of sin to be torn down. If they are to reclaim the lost relational territory that makes it possible to cleave in a "one-flesh" experience, it will be because they have laid down the guns of rebellion, and invited him to pave the way of the walk.

Obedient to his directions, they will ascend the moun-

CONCLUSION:
THE BOLD STROKE

Does marriage have an ultimate message? I am convinced that it does. If all relationships follow similar patterns and tend to differ only in degree of intensity, and if marriage is the most intimate and productive of all human relationships, it may have something to teach us about a man's relationship with his God.

There are marvelous parallels between the walk of man and wife and the walk of man and God. Both, for example, begin with *a sense of need.* "It is not good that man should be alone . . . ," God said. When God made that statement, man had a vertical relationship with God, but he had no horizontal relationship, and there was a void in his life. Later, because of sin, he would have the horizontal relationship, but he would have no vertical one. And because the vertical relationship was missing, the horizontal one would be terribly impaired.

Here is man or woman alone: that craving to have someone with whom life can be shared. If one is honest with himself, he will recognize an even deeper sense of need to know that he is in the right sort of communion with his Maker, God. For a time, a person can manage to muffle the sense of need that relational aloneness presents. Being busy, pursuing goals and achievements, or drowning one's thought process in a host of entertaining experiences can for a reasonably long time shut off the message of inner need for a lasting relationship. But the fact of emptiness has a way of popping to the top like a cork in that moment when we least expect it.

The horizontal aloneness—the need to find a person—will drive one to unbelievable lengths to fill the inner vacuum. I have seen men and women go to any extreme, overturning lifelong convictions and customs, virtually humiliating themselves to bridge the gap created through aloneness. Sooner or later the same quest begins on a spiritual level. At first, one may find contentment in thinking the vertical quest can be assuaged through a rigid code of personal ethics: being the *good* person; an exotic philosophy of life; some sort of meditative discipline; even, horror of horrors, a plain religious experience.

What kills our spirit, however, is the discovery at the end of the search that nothing quite works. There is always the burst of hope at the beginning that something adequate has been found; then the slow spiritual letdown: this wasn't it either.

The letdown comes because we are slow to learn the fact that man's aloneness is a relational problem, and it needs a relational answer. Philosophy, religion, meditation, and ethics are not relational in the sense that they provide a complete experience for the inner person. They provide something to do, something to think about, something to believe in, but they do not provide relationship.

Christianity is the story of God breaking through the relational barriers of rebellion to touch the life of a person through a work of Jesus Christ. In a specific sense, a person faces Jesus Christ in a time of spiritual need just as he faces a particular human being who he suspects will meet his human relational need.

How well I remember the letdowns on numerous occasions as a single young man. Like many, I often wondered if it were possible that I could actually love someone deeply for the rest of my life. But the greater question was, could there ever be someone who would love me? Each time I made a date with a new person, there was an aura of mystery and excitement. Would this be the one who would end the search, the one who would suddenly throw all the relays in my life-system and make a place in my heart? I can remember many premature affirmative answers. Convinced that this was the person, I would begin to fantasize the ultimate outcome; I was in love with love, more than I was in love with a person. Slowly the relationship would turn sour. Once again, I would be bewildered; is there no one to meet the need?

The world is full of people who have experienced a version or two of that kind of disappointment. But they have also faced it on the vertical, in the search for God. Momentary excitement that some system has been uncovered that brings fullness to life. But in the end a sour, stale taste: the letdown.

The Bible records the stories of many people who came to Jesus Christ with needs. There were momentary defeats, sloppy mistakes, and absurd ignorances, but there were no permanent letdowns. Peter thought the sky in his life had fallen when Christ died, but he was galvanized into action again when he discovered that Jesus had risen from death. Christianity, like marriage, brings to us an experience unlike anything else *when we acknowledge our need.*

I sit by the bed of my son one evening and find myself answering some of his questions about sex. Point by point his questions lead me down the path of a description of how mother and father experience love in the sexual experience. Convinced that the time has come for him to know the full story, I hold nothing back. His eleven-year-old mind intently takes it all in, and when I finish, he screws up his face, indicating a sense of revulsion. He assures me that nothing like that will ever happen in his lifetime. I smile inwardly and tell myself that in six years I'll be scared to death because his opinions on sex will be radically different. Why? Because an awareness of need will have arisen. There is no way right now that he will take seriously a relationship on the horizontal because he has no present sense of *need*. But when he finally matures and becomes aware of that *need*, *everything* will change.

Marriage takes us on to a second important lesson. Neither a potential partner in marriage (on the horizontal) or a potential Lord (on the vertical) can touch a person's life *until he is ready to make a commitment*. All the words I could muster up in praise of Gail were actually meaningless until one day I stepped down the aisle of a church and made a commitment. The commitment was, when you look at it on paper, rather undramatic. It consisted of a series of affirmations and promises. It was relatively simple to make; it hardly took into account the vast experiences that lay before the two of us after the wedding was over. It was a tiny threshold into a vast wonderland of relationships.

I shudder now when I realize how naive I was that day when I made my commitment to Gail. Perhaps if I had known the dimensions of the challenge of cleaving, I might have been more cautious, wondering if I could really meet the demands of marriage. Here was one time when ignorance may have been my friend.

The point of wedding day was simple: I put my convictions on the line and crossed it. I stopped saying nice things about Gail and committed my entire life to her. Nothing was held back, absolutely nothing. There was no unread fine print, no loopholes, no conditions. I was hers unreservedly, and she was mine. Our relationship had a formal beginning point to which we often look. If everything in our life together were suddenly to sour, we could still go back to the one point in time when our relationship came to the surface and was visible: the statement of our vows before God, the minister, and our friends. We even have a piece of paper which witnesses our assent to the relationship.

My Christian life had to have much the same beginning. There had to come a time in my experience with God where I unreservedly crossed a line. The New Testament has several words which it employs to describe what it means to cross that line into relationship with God. One is the word *receive;* another is the word *believe;* and still a third is *accept.* All are different faces of the same reality; one has to make a private and deliberate decision to lay down the rebellious attitude we all have by nature against the authority of God, and accept his lordship.

Many people are offended by the biblical word *sin,* and they resent being called sinners. There is no way to make one comfortable with the Bible's teaching about sin; the Scriptures are very blunt on the subject: everyone is a sinner. Trace the meaning of it, and you discover that what the Bible is saying is that a sinner is a rebel from the kingdom of God. He will always be a rebel, living in the fruits of rebellion until he alone makes a conscious decision to leave the war and lay down his arms. In most rebellions in history, rebels are punished severely, often executed. The Bible says that the penalty for rebellion against God *is* death, banishment from his presence. There would be no advantage in our laying down arms, therefore, except that God has provided a legal way for our sentence to be commuted. By dying on the cross, the Bible says, Jesus paid the penalty that every rebel is sentenced to pay for his rebellion.

The only decision really left to me is to lay down my rebellious lifestyle and accept the peace that God offers through the death of his Son, Jesus Christ. That act of surrender, crossing the line, is similar in magnitude and consequence to the act I made at the front of the church when I married Gail. As I gave her my life in human companionship, relinquishing all my rights, so I gave Christ my life. I say to both on their respective levels, "I give myself to you; I await the gift of your love; and I wish to become the kind of man each of you wishes me to be."

As the wedding ceremony was really quite uncomplicated and brief, my commitment to God was simple also. There were no tears, and there was no demonstrable action either on the part of Heaven or myself. I didn't cry; Heaven didn't parade a group of singing angels in the sky. There was only the quiet confidence that everything was under control, and that God had offered the promise of his love if I would surrender. I *believed* that God would do what he said; I *accepted* the gift of peace; I *received* the relationship Christ provided.

In both my marriage and my Christian life, there was *a brief period of emotional euphoria.* I distinctly remember the days of our honeymoon. We unashamedly announced to the world through car horns, streamers and tin cans, outlandish clothing, frequent embraces, polished rings, and enthusiastic smiles that we were in love. We could care less who knew it; in fact, the more the better. Honeymoons are unreal: pure emotional joy. Nothing is normal about them. Reality hits when you get home a few days later. The bathroom faucet is leaking; here is an unpaid bill; there is a schedule card that says the first class of the new year is at seven o'clock tomorrow morning. But, oh, the emotion of the honeymoon!

New Christians also go through a honeymoon period. They are so in love with the new lifestyle that they embarrass everyone about them. The old ways were getting stale and sour; they felt continual bondage and inner misery. Now all of that is gone; it's a new trip, and they tell the world about it. The Christian honeymoon can often last for months. Many older Christians look at new Christians in their honeymoon period and wish they could reclaim that joy. But they can't quite do it any more than a couple married for twenty years can honestly go back and reclaim the naive excitement of their honeymoon at Niagara Falls. They know too much, and their love has long passed the merely emotional level. We should not be surprised, if we are new Christians, that we are euphoric. During those times—as it is with new brides and grooms—we are full of promises and intentions. It never occurs to us that we could let God down. But we will . . . and we do.

The Christian has spiritual "leaky faucets," and he has "unpaid bills," and sooner or later the spiritual honeymoon comes to a kind of end. Now a person has to move on a day-to-day basis, cleaving to God in more ways than just through the emotions. Now the faith must be more than a "feel-good" faith; it must touch the mind and spirit and address itself to the hard questions of *knowing* and *living*. The honeymoon does end.

But if the honeymoon ends, it does not mean that cleaving is any less real. The fact is that the cleaving has gone subterranean; it matures and grows. In marriage, cleaving becomes broader and more meaningful because we spend more and more time together. Little by little our styles of life and our attitudes begin to change; we think alike, and we know what to expect from the other in crisis moments. We know each other's strengths and weaknesses. We are becoming one flesh, and life has changed for us.

There are quiet moments when all of us may look back to the single life, and we may fantasize for a moment on what it would be like to again be free. But then we realize, if we have effectively cleaved, that what we have in whole is far beyond what the uncommitted man may enjoy for fleeting moments. It is true that he enjoys a kind of fun; he has few commitments and responsibilities. But he *is* alone. And seeing that and recalling our former need we again appreciate the changes of living we have undergone. We have no desire to go back.

The Christian life is an act of cleaving. Walking in the steps of Christ clearly makes changes in our lifestyle. Paul writes, "We are being saved. . . ." Saved from what? The old style of life. Christ makes no mistakes;

177

the walk therefore always goes in his direction. We are the ones who bend and take the steps that he takes in relationship with people, moral decisions, and attitudes toward our work and its rewards. Life changes with Christ, and that led Paul to say, "If any man is in Christ [walking with him] he is a new creation." In a human sense, walking with my wife has virtually made me a new person; in the heavenly sense, walking with Christ has dramatically made me a new creation.

The relationships of marriage and Christian faith offer other parallels from which we can learn. They both have moments of *conflict*. Disagreement with Gail does not bring divorce or dissolution of the relationship. We took vows for life. It may mean silence, however, and it may mean some anger, hurt, and even the immature desire to fight back and slightly humiliate. When I get into conflict with Gail I begin to think like an unmarried man. I assert my individuality, and I think about myself—not necessarily about her. All my energies are directed toward vindicating *my* position, throwing up a wall to protect *my* integrity and dignity. In my attempt to make my case, I may even act like an unmarried man, showing her little or no consideration, certainly no affirmation or affection. She may be geographically approximate to me, but she might as well be a thousand miles away.

Legally we are married, but relationally we are out of touch with each other. It is the same with our walk with Christ. We are brothers with Christ after we cross the line. If one day we become unfaithful to him by a thought, an act of renewed rebellion, by a word of betrayal, there is nothing to indicate that Jesus cuts us off. Sinful acts will continue after one becomes a Christian. Hopefully, they will become less and less as we learn what Christ is asking of us, but there will always be moments when the bars are let down.

What happens? Is our Christian experience terminated? Does God disown us? Has Christ withdrawn his offer of peace? No way! Yes, there is silence, and we will not hear the voice of God speaking with much clarity. We certainly will not have much of a desire to speak to him. Cleaving is retarded, and it becomes as if God were also a thousand miles away. God isn't a thousand miles away any more than Gail is during conflict; it just *seems* that way.

What melts conflict? On both levels it is the same thing: *confession*. Confession in the context of love invites forgiveness. When I come home late for supper, and Gail is hurt, it is not a time for me to become indignant and try to avoid the responsibility. It is time for me to go to her, put my arms around her—if she'll let me—and tenderly and meaningfully say, "I'm sorry." The longer I wait, the harder it will be, and the more I'll have to say I'm sorry for. Being the kind of woman she usually is, she will respond to a sincere confession and forgive.

God responds to the prayer of the confessing Christian who faces up to the places where he has spiritually fallen flat on his face. It is a joy to know a loving God who says, "A righteous man falls seven (or an unlimited number of) times but gets up again." He gets up because we have a faithful Heavenly Father who responds to pleas for help and lifts us off our faces and sets us back into the right pattern of living again. Conflicts with God do not have to last long; my marriage has given me the precedent for seeing how that can be true.

Both my marriage and my Christian experience have *intimate moments*. In the privacy of our relationships, Gail and I share affection apart from everyone else, and we become one flesh. It is a precious time, and it sums up the entire drama of our relationship. It looks both *backward* to what we have become to one another, and *forward* as it affirms our pledged unity for events in the future. In the *present* it brings peace to our minds and bodies. The tensions are relaxed, and in each other's arms we find a kind of tranquillity which the world cannot duplicate.

A person shares intimacies of a similar nature with

God. Jesus suggested that there was a time for an experience in the "closet." That is that quiet time when, as in marriage, a person confesses and gives thanks for past mistakes and victories, intercedes for the challenges of the future, and rejoices in the confidence of an ever-present God. Finally one relaxes in the present and enjoys the knowledge that God is with him. "I shall be his God, and he shall be my son," God says. Intimacy with God is a privilege of the Christian life.

It is from that entire experience of cleaving and progressive one-fleshedness that certain results spring. God has allowed Gail and me to share two lovely children, the result of our lives together. They resemble us not only physically, but in personality. This both gladdens me and saddens me. Nevertheless, they are the product of our relationship. Beyond them, our lives together have spawned many spiritual children, some of whom are on the mission field, some in pastorates, some in business and laboring positions. Depending upon the amount of contact we have had with them, they bear the marks of our discipleship. Often we have grinned as we have heard them employ favorite words of ours in their prayers. We have heard them communicate with others in concepts which we have taught them. We have seen them cope in crisis according to the principles we have given them. And it is the greatest satisfaction we have: to have borne children physically and spiritually.

Cleaving with God is always *productive*. No one becomes a Christian for the sheer status of being a member of the Heavenly family. God calls us to himself that he might make us into something productive. The greatest mark of our relationship to him is that something is produced in our lives that could not have been produced without that mutual communion. Every person in the Bible who gave his or her life to God became something significant in service. Not everyone becomes a preacher or missionary; these are not necessarily first-class jobs while others are second-class. Rather, *all* of us are mutually significant to God; and *all* of us are expected to bear witness to our relationship with him. From our relationship, there is the emergence of spiritual children, people who are compelled to come to him because they have seen the love of Christ in us.

There are two more important considerations in the matter of the parallel between marriage and the Church. The first is the matter of productivity. I am convinced that the greatest mistake many Christians are making both in their lives with God and with their spouses is their unawareness of the ultimate objective of those relationships. *The objective of relationship is servant-hood.* Almost every Christian would agree that we enter into marriage to *give* rather than to *get.* Yet we often make the shortsighted error of thinking that one enters into the Christian life only to *get,* to be *blessed,* to have *good feelings,* or to be *secure.* It is that tendency which non-Christians often take us to task about. They sense that we are just on a "trip," looking out for what is best for us.

Too often, for example, we go to worship services with that intention: what can *I* get out of it? We even go to God with the subtle objective, "*I want* to grow." Little do we realize that all that we seek is received in fullness when we take the first step of giving everything of ourselves as servants. It is one of God's functions to make people into servants. We take our place with the lowest of the low, and we approach every relationship with the question, how can I help? How can I give? How can I encourage? How can I build? What a dramatically different mentality Christ wishes to place within us than the one that always asks, "What's in this for me?"

The final important thought has been expressed throughout this book in a dozen different ways. We must recognize that there is one who will do everything in his power to destroy the relationships we are building on both the horizontal and vertical planes. If the evil one cannot destroy the relationship, then he will resort to jamming the lines of communication and dulling the joys as much as possible. As Paul once told the church, "Be watchful and alert." Marriage is, like our Christian experience, a supernatural life. Its success will depend upon our openness to God's Spirit so that we can discern both opportunities to serve, and dangers which will separate.

Now perhaps you see why marriage is exciting, not only because it fulfills the relational void and solves aloneness, but because it is a bold stroke of witness. The Christ-oriented relationship is a cup of cool water in a society where relationships grow increasingly sterile. Where there is relationship, there is life. And people are hungry to know life. They have exhausted themselves "living," and they have found no life. They have exploited knowledge, but found no truth. They have established many acquaintances, but have few relationships.

A marriage where romance, companionship, servanthood are all oriented to Jesus Christ will bring people to one flesh, and wherever that happens the world will sit up and take notice. A few will try to discredit it; some will envy it. But many will come to bask in its light and take away a new understanding of what God may have for them.

NOTES

1. Used by permission of *Christian Medical Society Journal*, Oak Park, Ill.

2. Used by permission of Field Newspaper Syndicate.

3. Esther Howard, *Faith at Work*, June 1974.

4. Walter Trobisch, *I Married You* (New York: Harper & Row, 1971), p. 119.

5. Paul Tournier, *To Understand Each Other* (© 1967 by M. E. Bratcher and used by permission of John Knox Press, Atlanta, Ga.).

6. C. S. Lewis, *A Grief Observed* (© 1961 by N. W. Clerk and used by permission of The Seabury Press, Inc., New York), n.p.

7. *Ibid.*

8. *Ibid.*

9. Trobisch, *I Married You*, p. 119.

10. Blake Clark, "Your Emotions Can Make You Ill," *Reader's Digest*, May 1972, © by The Reader's Digest Association, Inc., Pleasantville, NY.

11. Jay Adams, *Christian Living in the Home* (Nutley, N.J.: Presbyterian and Reformed Publishing House), n.p.

12. John Pollock, *Hudson Taylor and Maria* (© by Curtis Brown, New York).

13. Trobisch, *I Married You*, p. 50.

14. Used by permission of Abigail VanBuren.

15. Taken from *Song and Garden Birds of North America*, by permission of National Geographic Society, Washington, D.C.

16. Carolyn Davies, "Diary of a Mad Housewife," *The Wittenburg Door*, San Diego, Calif.

17. Emile Cailliet, *Alone at High Noon* (Grand Rapids, Mich.: Zondervan Publishing House, 1971), p. 34.